PRAISE FOR

Dr. Kaiser powerfully exposes the relational and theological wreckage caused to the Jewish people by Christians promoting replacement theology. Walking carefully through history and the Bible, he demonstrates how the Jews retain the promises provided in the unconditional Abrahammic Covenant and, contrary to the beliefs of many, how the church has not usurped God's covenant people. I loudly applaud his work and hope it gains a deep foothold in the pulpits and pews of the western church.

J. Paul Nyquist, Ph.D., President, Moody Bible Institute

How did Jewish and Gentile Christians who are both linked to the same covenants of promise and Messiah become so separated from each other with such awful consequences? Walter Kaiser offers a very helpful and much needed answer to this question. This book is loaded with significant historical and theological content as Kaiser works the reader step-by-step through how Jewish and Gentile allies in Jesus the Messiah eventually became so separated from each other. Hopefully the insight this book brings will be a corrective against current replacement theology and supersessionism against Israel that still doggedly remains in the Christian church. This book is must reading, and so interesting I had to read it in one sitting.

Michael J. Vlach, Ph.D., Professor of Theology, The Master's Seminary

Sadly, divisiveness and misunderstanding have often characterized the long history of Jewish-Christian relations. From his seasoned Christian perspective, Walter Kaiser effectively draws upon biblical, theological and historical sources to help clarify some of the more perplexing issues. The author deftly explains the vocation of Israel is far from over through his well-argued case against replacement theology. This book will challenge every serious reader to think anew about Jew and Gentile in the plan of God.

Marvin R. Wilson, Ph.D., H. J. Ockenga Professor of Biblical and Theological Studies, Gordon College

Dr. Walter Kaiser has been a gift to the body of Christ and especially to the Messianic Jewish community and those who love the Jews. His passion for the Word and his love for my people Israel have made him to be one of my favorite scholars and Bible teachers of all time. His latest book *Jewish Christianity: Why Believing Jews and Gentiles Parted Ways in the Early Church,* is a marvelous addition to his already rich body of work. Most appreciated in this book is Kaiser's call to repudiate replacement theology and to make the theology of Israel and the Jewish people a part of Christian theology. His chapters on history will shed additional light on the place of Jewish believers in Jesus, or the lack of them, in church history. If more people would read this book by Dr. Kaiser, the Church would be enriched to better understand her roots, Jewish believers would feel more welcomed in the body of Christ and perhaps, just perhaps, more of my Jewish people would come to embrace their Messiah Yeshua (Jesus).

David Brickner, M.A., Executive Director, Jews for Jesus

Walt Kaiser is an extremist in the minds of some who hold to replacement theology. When he comes to the word *Israel,* he understands it as *Israel!* Many details from the book will be debated even by Christian Zionists such as the precise nature of the relationship of Israel and the Church theologically and historically. Nonetheless, *Jewish Christianity* offers a refreshing commitment to literal interpretation and a rebuttal of replacement theology found in Roman Catholicism and in Reformed Christianity. The Church simply does not assume the promises to the nation of Israel in an allegorical way. While many others have championed the same points, the uniqueness of Kaiser's work is the historical outline of Jewish Christianity covering the past two thousand years. In this way, he helps to fill in many gaps overlooked in historical as well as theological understanding. Kaiser's final challenge to all of us is to consider the theological significance of the Holocaust and the restoration of Israel as a nation in 1948 in view of the Bible's teaching about the Jewish people and national Israel.

Mike Stallard, Ph.D., Director of International Ministry, Friends of Israel Gospel Ministry

Walter Kaiser writes with wisdom, wit, and insight. His new book on *Jewish Christianity* provides a biblical, historical, and practical look at the Jewish roots of the Christian faith. He exposes the weaknesses of "replacement theology," while making the case for Christian support for Israel. Don't miss this powerful and helpful study.

Dr. Ed Hindson, Founding Dean and Distinguished Professor, Rawings School of Divinity, Liberty University

There is a growing biblical and historical challenge today confronting replacement theology, that is supercessionism. This shameful blot on Christendom is vigorously engaged by such a splendid volume as *Jewish Christianity*. Here are the indisputible Hebrew roots of Christianity, they being upheld with great facility. After all, will not Jesus return as the quintessential Jew? Here is a further scholarly broadside that challenges the anti-Judaism prevalent in our day. May it be blessed in enlightening those who earnestly desire to understand the abiding Hebrew roots of the Christian faith.

Barry E. Horner, D.Min., Author of *Future Israel*

As always, Dr. Walter Kaiser provides us a solid and scholarly exposition of Jews and Gentiles in the plan of God. Deep into the Scriptures and the eternal plan of God, Kaiser continues to enrich God's people with this study of His immutable promises. Highly recommended.

Dr. David L. Larsen, Professor Emeritus, Trinity Evangelical Divinity School, Deerfield, Illinois

Professor Walt Kaiser has been a mentor and a boss to me. I am convinced firsthand that his approach to the biblical text is not only thoughtful and intellectually grounded, but is also steeped in wisdom and practical guidance on important issues of the day. In all of his scholarship I have read—and he has written much—he is a careful scholar and articulate writer. He practices what he preaches. If you are interested in the important conversation about the history of believing Jews and Gentiles, then you can count on this book as one more in the long line of Walt Kaiser's writings that will inform and inspire.

Barry H. Corey, Ph.D., President of Biola University and author of *Love Kindness: Discover the Power of a Forgotten Christian Virtue*

The great historic divide between Christians and Jews has far deeper roots than you may have imagined. Thanks to Walt Kaiser who has traced the history back to the early years of the church to open up new vistas of understanding that will enable us to have a more sensitive attitude and sympathetic perspective. This is a fascinating read that turns the lights on in a dark room of our past.

Dr. Joe Stowell, President, Cornerstone University, Grand Rapids, Michigan

As a Jewish follower of Jesus, I wish all believers would read Dr. Kaiser's informative and insightful book. Not only does Dr. Kaiser provide a helpful history of Jewish believers but he also illuminates the place of the Jewish people in biblical promise and prophecy. Dr. Kaiser's strong correction to the church's current fascination with supersessionism should be essential reading for every believer.

Dr. Michael Rydelnik, Professor of Jewish Studies and Bible, Moody Bible Institute, Nationally Syndicated Radio Host/Bible Teacher *Open Line with Dr. Michael Rydelnik*, Co-Editor and Contributor *The Moody Bible Commentary*

In just over one hundred pages, Walt Kaiser has bestowed a gift on the church of immeasurable value. *Jewish Christianity: Why Believing Jews and Gentiles Parted Ways in the Early Church* is a magnificent insight into the social, political and religious forces which assailed the church at the close of the First century and into the second and third centuries. Kaiser speaks to the development of the doctrine of Supersessionism or Replacement theology in the thinking of many churches and denominations. While evaluating those perspectives and theologians with kindness and respect, Kaiser demonstrates how hurtful Replacement theology has been and how exegetically flawed it is. If you wish to read one book that will change your perspective regarding God's purpose for Israel, read this book.

Dr. Paige Patterson, President, Southwestern Baptist Theological Seminary, Fort Worth, Texas

JEWISH CHRISTIANITY

WHY BELIEVING JEWS AND GENTILES PARTED WAYS IN THE EARLY CHURCH

WALTER C. KAISER, JR.

Jewish Christianity
Copyright © 2017 Walter C. Kaiser, Jr.
All rights reserved.

No part of this book may be reproduced in any form or by any electronic or mechanical means including information storage and retrieval systems, without permission in writing from the author. The only exception is by a reviewer, who may quote short excerpts in a review.

Lampion Press, LLC
P.O. Box 932
Silverton, OR 97381

ISBN: 978-1-942614-29-6
Library of Congress Control Number: 2017944805

Formatting and cover design by Amy Cole, JPL Design Solutions

Printed in the United States of America

ACKNOWLEDGEMENTS

Special thanks and appreciation must be expressed to my good friend and servant of Christ, Dr. Hershel Wayne House and the work of the new Lampion Press. His suggestions and comments have made this work a better piece than it ordinarily would have been. I am also deeply grateful for the editorial work of Carrie Stanley and Tim Demy, the design work of Amy Cole, and Irina House for procuring dedications. As always, this work is offered "To the glory of God

**FOR ALL WHO HAVE MINISTERED
SO FAITHFULLY IN THE SERVICE OF
MESSIAH AMONG THE JEWISH FAMILY
AROUND THE GLOBE.**

TABLE OF CONTENTS

Introduction 3

CHAPTER 1: When Believing Jewish Persons
and Believing Gentiles were One in Messiah 7

CHAPTER 2: When Supersessionism and
Replacement Theology Drew Up Lines 21

CHAPTER 3: When the Christian Church Needs
Israel and Israel Needs the Church 37

CHAPTER 4: When the Relationship Between the Israel
and the New Christian Church of the
Abrahamic-Davidic Covenant went Sour 51

CHAPTER 5: When John the Baptist Prepared
the "Way" for Yeshua 67

CHAPTER 6: When the Jewish and
Gentile Christians Fled to Pella 77

CHAPTER 7: When the Community of
Jewish Christians Slowly Fell Apart 83

CHAPTER 8: When the Effects of Replacement
Theology are Realized in our Systematic Theology 97

Bibliography 109

INTRODUCTION

The term "Jewish Christians" sounds like an oxymoron, but it really does have its roots in a very important period in the early history and beginnings of Christianity. In fact, the earliest days of these Jewish Christians came in the first Christian century, when the first group of believers was mostly Jewish followers of Yeshua (i.e., "Jesus") the Messiah. Yes, this company of Jewish people did include a small number of Gentiles, but they made up a minority of the group that originally was called followers of the "Way." The majority of those who followed Yeshua certainly were Jewish as we learn from the book of Acts as the followers of the "Way" increased.

The origin of these followers of the Way began at Pentecost, where as a result of the preaching of the apostle Peter, some 3,000 Jewish men and women (Acts 2:41) professed their faith in Yeshua. It was this same Yeshua who just 50 days prior had demonstrated that He was the true Son of God, indeed the Messiah Himself, by rising from the dead on Easter Sunday morning after being in the grave Friday evening, all day Saturday and part of Sunday morning.[1] Later the number of Jewish men who believed in Yeshua grew by another 5,000 (Acts 4:4). So the work that began on Pentecost was, from the start, marked by an enormous number of those who were descendants of Abraham, Isaac, Jacob, Moses and David, and they formed the overwhelming majority who make up what was called in those days, "The Way." This movement continued to

---

1 Matthew 28, Mark 16, Luke 24, John 20.

grow exponentially as the hand of God was most evident in the witnessing and work of this early company of believers.

There still was no New Testament available at this time, for these additions to the existing canon of Scripture at that time (the Tanach, i.e., the Old Testament) did not come until the book of James and Paul's letter to the Galatians first appeared between A.D. 46–48. After that, the apostle Paul began to contribute one epistle after another under divine inspiration as a gift to newly formed companies of believers in city after city in the 50s and 60s. He wrote the epistles of 1 and 2 Thessalonians, 1 and 2 Corinthians, and the book of Romans in the A.D. 50s. The early 60s were marked by four of Paul's letters, Colossians, Philemon, Ephesians, and Philippians, which he wrote from prison. Their purpose was to edify the newly formed "churches."

The Gospels of Matthew and Mark were written in the middle of the 60s, followed by the two-volume history by Paul's traveling companion, the physician Luke, known as Luke and Acts. Then 1 and 2 Peter and Jude also came about A.D. 64–65, followed by the Pastoral Epistles from Paul (1 and 2 Timothy and Titus) toward the end of that same decade. Somewhere around this same time the book of Hebrews appeared, but its author remains a mystery to this day, despite a large number of contenders for the honor, along with a wide assortment of guesses.

This first common, or Christian, century concluded with the writings of the apostle John. In the ninth decade of this first century A.D., he wrote the Gospel of John, 1, 2 and 3 John and the book of Revelation. The canon of Scripture that contained all 66 books surely would be completed by the second century A.D.[2]

But even before God had sent this written revelation of His will, He had given it in the person of Yeshua and His works in the three years of his ministry just prior to His death and resurrection. That, along with the prompting of the Holy Spirit, had begun to introduce large numbers of believers—many of whom were Jewish—into the joy of their salvation.

---

2   The Council of Jamnia (or Yavneh in Hebrew) officially recognized the 39 books of the Old Testament as authoritative in A.D 90, while the list prepared by Athanasius in his 39th festal letter for the church in Alexandria are the same 27 books of the New Testament now recognized by the Protestant movement as authoritative. See Gregg R. Allison, *Historical Theology: An Introduction to Christian Doctrine* (Grand Rapids: Zondervan, 2011), 37-58.

Along with the growing number of Jewish people who responded to this descendant of King David as the promised Messiah, there were many Gentiles who also were joining them in belief in this Yeshua. It was an exciting time for the new converts, whether Jew or Gentile.

But in the midst of all the enthusiasm over this enlarged and fast growing number of the "people of God," made up of Jews and Gentiles, there came a sudden crisis in A.D. 50 that threatened to tear apart all the good groundwork that had been laid by Yeshua and His apostles. This crisis revolved around the issue of *how* Gentiles were to be accepted into the mainly Jewish fellowship. The more conservative Jewish Christians felt that they should be received on the same basis that Jews had always accepted Gentiles into the covenant community—through proselyte initiation.[3] The conflict came to a head around A.D. 50 at the Jerusalem Council (Acts 15) as a result of inquiries that had been made from an increasing number of Gentile believers now joining this group from up north in Syrian Antioch. Some of them did not submit to all the distinctives found in the Jewish Law of Moses, and the problem threatened to turn into a racial, as well as a theological, problem for this young group. The council reached a good solution in Acts 15:20, and the two ethnic groups continued to worship and serve the Lord side by side for another eighty-five years. However, the strength and presence of a proportionately larger group of Jewish people in this fellowship of the "Way" can be seen in the fact that according to Jerome, the first fifteen bishops in Jerusalem of this new group were all Jewish until A.D. 135.[4]

The Roman conquest of Jerusalem in A.D. 70 had dramatically changed much in the land of Israel in regards to Jewish Christianity (such as movement from the temple to pervasive influence of the Rabbinate and the gradual alienation of Jewish Christians from the synagogue). But what really altered the relationship between Jewish Christianity and the broader Jewish community, as well as the Jews and Rome, was the fact that a certain Jewish man, who was called Bar Kochba, laid a claim to his

---

3   John B. Polhill, *Acts*, Vol. 26, NAC (Nashville: Broadman & Holman, 1992), 321.

4   Jerome, *Catalogue of Ecclesiastical* 4.5. Eusebius, *The Church History of Eusebius IV*, in *Nicene and Post-Nicene Fathers of the Christian Church*, Vol. 1, ed. Henry Wace and Philip Schaff (Oxford: Parker and Company, 1890), 176.

being the Messiah. This outrageous claim was surprisingly supported by the influential Rabbi Akiba.[5] However, Bar Kochba's Jewish followers suffered a second devastating defeat for the sons of Israel at the hands of the Romans in A.D. 135, and thereby raised a cautionary flag for anyone else who had claimed to be a "Messiah," such as included Yeshua. This slowed down the growth of the Jewish segment in this group, but it apparently had little or no effect on the Gentile growth at that time.

All of this was enough to account for the rocky relations between the Jewish and Gentile believers, but as early as the second Christian century, there began to appear an anti-Semitic sentiment starting with Justin Martyr, a second-century Church Father, who began to speak incautiously about the Jewish people at large and their rejection of the Jewish Messiah. Justin Martyr's *Dialogue with Trypho* initiated a long diatribe against the Jewish people from the pens of Christian writers that would bring dishonor to the Gentile believers and shame to the cause of Christ.[6] It would continue and eventually lead all the way up to the Holocaust, as subsequent information will demonstrate.

In what follows, we have tried to trace some of this history of ill-will between the two sides and to show especially how the emergence of the view that later became known as known as "replacement theology" did much damage to evangelistic efforts among the Jewish people, as well as an outright rejection of the eternal promise-plan of God that had been made with the Jewish people through Abraham, Isaac, and Jacob. This will call for a careful reading of both the historical and biblical records, for both are affected by the appearance of this view, which will also be known as "supersessionism."

May our Lord grant us the understanding to revisit the historical and biblical records once again, and we ask our Lord for forgiveness and a determination to treat the Jewish people in an altogether different sort of manner as we seek to see His promise in a whole new light.

---

5   Walter A. Elwell and Barry J. Beitzel, *Baker Encyclopedia of the Bible* (Grand Rapids, MI: Baker, 1988), 47.

6   T. J. Horner, *Listening to* Trypho: *Justin Martyr's Dialogue Reconsidered* (Leuven: LUP, 2001).

CHAPTER 1

WHEN BELIEVING JEWISH PERSONS AND BELIEVING GENTILES WERE ONE IN MESSIAH[7]

☙

When it comes to describing the relationships between Jewish and Gentile believers in Messiah during the first common Christian century, most traditional Rabbinic and Christian theology emphasize the complete distinction and separation between the synagogue and the church. Yet, it turns out that this conclusion suffers from a huge historic distortion and lapse of memory about how events actually happened in those early days of the first common century as a result of Yeshua's (henceforth the Jewish name for Jesus) three-year ministry in Israel and the follow-up done by the apostolic witness.

At the start of the first common/Christian century (C.E. = A.D.), the good news announced by Yeshua's followers found a natural home with a surprisingly large number of Messianic believers in the Jewish community and in a large number of the synagogues. So responsive was the Jewish audience to the gospel at first that they made up the larger number of those who put their trust in Yeshua as their personal Messiah and thus became part of the "Way." This situation continued perhaps up to the beginning of the second Christian century. In this way, a warm relationship between

---

[7] This chapter is an enlargement of a lecture first given at the "Gershom Lectures in Jewish-Christian Relationships" at Hillsdale College, January 19–21, 2014. A slightly revised version of these lectures was given as the "Robert Cooley Lectures" at Gordon-Conwell Theological Seminary, Charlotte, NC on January 15–16, 2015.

Jewish and Gentile converts began the formation of a new unity in Yeshua and in a community of all believers in Yeshua the Messiah.[8]

THE INITIATION OF JEWISH-CHRISTIAN AND GENTILE BELIEVERS' RELATIONS

Let us start from the beginning, in fact, at the most important point in this discussion. We must begin by noting that Yeshua of Nazareth certainly was not of any Gentile extraction or heritage, for He was born a Jew. What is more, Yeshua was circumcised the eighth day according to the Mosaic Law (Luke 2:21), and he received a Jewish name ("Yeshua," also rendered "Jesus," which is a transliteration through the Latin and Greek of the Hebrew "Jehoshua" or "Joshua," meaning "[Yahweh] will save [his people from their sins]," Matt 1:21). His historical origins were rooted in the flesh of a Jewish genealogy, marking him as "the Son of Abraham" and "the Son of David" in a list of relatives' names in Matthew's Gospel that focused on the number "fourteen" for its organization and presentation of the genealogy (Matt 1:17), which is the numerical value of the Hebrew consonants in the name of "David" (D = 4, W/V = 6; D + V + D = 14). Moreover, Yeshua also had the appearance of a Jewish person (not like the Christian pictures of a blue-eyed Teutonic blond). He lived in the cities of Nazareth and Capernaum in Galilee and read the Tanach (= O.T.) with His Jewish parents and teachers (Luke 2:41–47), as He also spoke one of the Jewish languages of that day, Aramaic, as hinted at by His use of such Aramaic words as *"Abba"* ("Father," Mark 14:36), or when He performed a miracle with the Aramaic order to the dead young girl, *"Talitha cum"* ("Little girl, get up," Mark 5:41), or finally as he cried out in Aramaic on the cross, *"Eli, Eli, lama sabachthani?"* ("My God, my God, why have you forsaken me?" Matt 27:46). Therefore, Yeshua was most assuredly and distinctively Jewish as to his human origins.

It was this same Yeshua, however, who announced to Peter, "I will build my Church" (Matt 16:18) as he appointed twelve Jewish disciples as the very foundation blocks of this new spiritual edifice, which He later

---

8   Daniel C. Harlow, "Early Judaism and Early Christianity," in *Early Judaism: A Comprehensive Review*, ed. John J. Collins and Daniel C. Harlow (Grand Rapids: Eerdmans, 2012), 391-419; Cp. *Mart. Poly.* 10. Cp. Ignatius, *Magnesians* 9.1, 10.1-3.

called the "church" (Eph 2:19–22). Thus, at Pentecost, this same new work of God was announced before a Jerusalem throng that was essentially, if not entirely, Jewish (Acts 1:2–2:4). At this event, about 3,000 male and female Jewish believers made up the first fellowship of this new group, much later to be called the "church," as Jerusalem became the mother congregation that continued to gather into her fold an overwhelming number of Jewish believers, joined by a lesser number of Gentile believers.

Afterwards severe tensions, and some persecution, broke out against this believing community in Jerusalem from the likes of a strict Pharisee named "Saul," who was later renamed "Paul" after his conversion (later named an apostle). This resulted in the scattering of the believers throughout the land of Judah and Samaria (Acts 8:1). But the astonishing factor was that this group also began to include hybrid believers from Samaria, for the Samaritans were already ethnically mixed, partly Jewish and partly Gentile (Acts 8:4–17), by edict from the conquering Assyrians back in 721 B.C.[9] This group was later followed by Gentile believers who came from Caesarea, the city by the Mediterranean Sea (Acts 10:1–48) built by Herod the Great between 22 and 10 B.C. and dedicated to Caesar. With such ethnic diversity the scene in the believing body was set for both growth, along with the potential for some tensions, as Jewish and Gentile believers began to meet together to reconcile their differences over the law. In fact, this tension came not from the outside the group alone, but it also began to arise from within the believing fellowship as well, for by the year A.D. 50, the Council of Jerusalem, in full agreement with the apostles Peter and Paul, decided that the Gentile Christians living up north in Antioch, should not be required to submit to all the distinctive ceremonial rituals, including circumcision, in Judaism so long as: (1) they abstained from food polluted by idols, (2) did not engage in sexual immorality, (3) did not eat blood or (4) they did not eat meat from strangled animals (Acts 15:20). Most importantly, they believed that by faith in Yeshua as the Son of God, who died and rose again for their sins, these Gentiles could be redeemed—exactly how the Jewish believers were saved as well!

---

9 See Gary N. Knoppers, *Jews and Samaritans: The Origins and History of Their Early Relations* (Oxford: Oxford University Press, 2013), 75-92.

Nevertheless, a good deal of concord between these two groups of believers continued to exist for about another eighty-five years, as evidenced by the fact that the first fifteen bishops over this new fellowship that would become the church in Jerusalem all were Jewish in ethnic background up to A.D. 135, according to Eusebius.[10] The evidence for any other ensuing tensions during this period, such as what might have occurred or how they were resolved, is not known to us in detail beyond what we get in Acts 15 and scraps of information from other writers in this period before the Common Era 135 (A.D.).

Some insight into how the Jerusalem Church understood itself can be gathered from the designations this new movement gave to itself. For example, the favored term Jewish believers used to identify themselves at first, was simply followers of "the Way." This title occurs five times in the book of Acts (Acts 9:2; 19:9, 23; 24:14, 22; also cf. 22:4). But we also find "the Way of the Lord" (18:25) and "the Way of God" (18:26). This form of identifying themselves likely came from its usage in Isaiah 40:3, where it was prophesied that John the Baptist (see below for the chapter on John the Baptist for more detail) was later to be given the task of "prepar[ing] *the way* of Yahweh, mak[ing] straight in the desert a highway for our God" (emphases mine). It is possible to add to this the eschatological references in the book of Isaiah, where God's salvation was called "the *Way* of my people" (57:14) or the "Holy *Way*" (35:8). For a number of years, the believing Jews and Gentiles of the "Way" viewed Jerusalem as their home base and perhaps the mother church of them all.

THE INFLUENCE OF JEWISH BELIEVERS IN THE CHURCH AT ROME [11]

This Jewish fellowship, established some years later in the capital of the Roman Empire, was bound to take some sort of leadership role for other groups following the way in the days that followed, since Rome was the

---

10 Eusebius. *Ecclesiastical History*, 4.5.

11 For this section, I am beholden to the fine work of Reidar Hvalvik, "Jewish Believers and Jewish Influence in the Roman Church until the Early Second Century," in *The Early Centuries: Jewish Believers in Jesus*, ed. Oskar Skarsaune and Reidar Hvalvik (Peabody, MA: Hendrickson Publishers, 2007), 179- 216, especially 180-90.

capital of the Roman Empire. Tradition has it that two Jewish leaders, the apostle Paul and the apostle Peter, were closely connected to the ministry of the fellowship in Rome at some point in that first Christian century. The apocryphal work of *Acts of Peter*, a non-canonical source, told about Paul coming to Rome, where he served as a shepherd of the congregation. After a time, Paul left Rome because he sensed a call to go to Spain, so the congregation bid farewell to the shepherd of their gathering, as they also presumably equipped and outfitted him for his forthcoming ministry.

However, after Paul left, a heretic by the name of Simon Magus arrived in Rome and began leading the believers astray by his teachings. It was for this reason that Peter was summoned to come to Rome, where he successfully fought Simon and led a fruitful teaching ministry, which was accompanied by many miracles. The story, however, ended with Peter being martyred crucified upside down, sometime in the late 60s.

We are never given any details on how or when the church at Rome was founded, as we are told, for example, about the establishment of the church at Corinth. Accordingly, we are supplied with an interesting piece of information in connection with Paul's arrival in Corinth in the spring of A.D. 50. When Paul arrived in Corinth, he met a Jewish man named Aquila, a native of Pontus, along with his wife Priscilla, both who had recently come from Rome because Caesar Claudius had ordered all Jews to leave the capital city of the Roman Empire. Paul went to meet this dynamic duo, and because both they and Paul were tentmakers, Paul stayed with them (Acts 18:2–3). This Jewish couple along with the other Jewish people had been expelled from Rome during its time of great civil turmoil; however, the key question was this: Was this turmoil the same episode that the Roman historian Suetonius wrote about in *De vita Caesarum*?[12] Regarding Claudius Caesar, Suetonius had written, "Since the Jews constantly made disturbances at the instigation of Chrestus, he expelled them from Rome." Though some are very loath to identify Claudius' use of "Chrestus" with "Christ" (i.e., as a misspelling for the Greek "Christus"), it is most likely that "Christ" is the one he had wanted to indicate in his decree of extradition of the Jewish people. In contradiction to such a claim, however, some point to the fact that Claudius' decree

---

12 *Divus Claudius* 25.4

came at an earlier date—C.E. 41, which would have placed Claudius' decree in the first year of his reign.[13] But this citation seems to be about an earlier edict from Claudius Caesar, for it came from another Roman historian by the name of Dio Cassius (c. A.D. 160–230), who specifically noted that Claudius "did not drive out" the Jewish people, but only ordered them not to hold their meetings. However, in a much later source,[14] about which Paulus Orosius writes: "In the ninth year [of Claudius]" the Jews were expelled from Rome. Even though Orosius incorrectly attributed his information to Josephus, that mistake did not exclude the possibility that he may nevertheless have been right in his dating of this event, which he set between 25 January 49 C.E. and 25 January 50 C.E., for Paul did arrive in Corinth in the spring of A.D. 50. If all of this were correctly argued, then it would appear that there were Jewish believers in Rome already in the A.D. 40s. It is important to realize that Claudius had also noted that this was something that was "constantly" going on, so the Jewish community in Rome may have been in a rather constant state of turmoil and uproar over who was this "Christ" and whether he was the long awaited Messiah.

The believers at Rome clearly showed they were made up of both Jews and Gentiles and that they were well taught by the likes of Paul and Peter. When Paul writes the letter to the Romans, his audience is made up of both Jewish and Gentile believers. The Jews who were expelled from Rome by Claudius are now back. However, they were the minority in the church, with the majority made up for believers that came from a pagan, Gentile background.[15]

PAUL'S RELATIONSHIP TO THE SYNAGOGUE

Since seventeen of the twenty-eight chapters in the book of Acts are dedicated to the story of the apostle Paul (Acts 9, 13–28), it could well be called "the book of Paul." Yet Paul began his career as a zealous Jew who bitterly opposed and persecuted the first believers in Yeshua. But all of that

---

13 Barbara Levick, *Claudius* (New Haven: Yale University Press, 1990), 37-38.

14 Paulus Orosius. *Historia adversus Paganos*, published in 417/18, 7.6.

15 Thomas R. Schreiner, *Romans,* BECNT (Grand Rapids: Baker, 1998), 10-14.

was about to dramatically change, for on Paul's journey to Damascus to carry out some of the authorized Jewish hostility against those who were following the "Way," which he had been granted by some of Jerusalem's Jewish leadership, he experienced a radical conversion. This God-initiated miracle changed his identity, and from that time forward he would be known as a follower of Yeshua, and a preacher of the good news that Yeshua was the long-expected Messiah (Gal 1:23).

A small debate, unfortunately, has recently broken out over the three versions of Paul's Damascus Road conversion experience (in Acts 9, 22, and 26)—some wanting to emphasize the "conversional" aspect of this Damascus Road event and others wanting to stress the fact that this was a typical "call" story. The truth is that both elements were present in what happened to this former hostile enemy of the gospel, for he experienced both a conversion from his sin and offensive guilt as well as a call to serve God at the same time. For some observers, "conversion" usually means an exchange of one religion for another, such as a change from Judaism to Christianity, but such terminology would be anachronistic, since there was no official religion named "Christianity" at this time. Moreover, it would not fit other facts as well, for the apostle Paul continued his relationship with the synagogue by making it his habit to go to preach in the synagogue first in almost every city where he went.

In this way, Paul continued to show his loyalty to his own ethnic background by adopting this procedure of preaching in each city's synagogue first, for this was his missionary method of presenting the gospel in every town where he landed (e.g. Acts 14:1). This was Paul's way of showing what he meant when he said that the gospel was the power of God, "to the Jews first" (e.g., Rom 1:16).

Nevertheless, E. P. Sanders asserted that the picture of Paul in Acts is not in accord with the picture we get from the same apostle in his epistles. In Acts, Paul is the teacher of Israel, but in the Pauline letters, he is the apostle to the Gentiles.[16] But such a strict division of labor is not borne out by the evidence. It is true, of course, that it was indeed Paul's habit first to visit the synagogue in order to preach the good news in almost every city he entered (Acts 13:14; 14:1; 17:1–2, 10, 17;

---

16 E. P. Sanders. *Paul, the Law and the Jewish People* (Philadelphia: Fortress, 1983), 181, 190.

18:4–6, 19; 19:8–9). From the preceding list of passages, this method and practice of Paul would fit this practice of preaching in the cities of Pisidian Antioch, Iconium, Thessalonica, Berea, Athens, Corinth, and Ephesus. Accordingly, the result of this procedure was as follows: Paul would enter the city and begin preaching in the synagogue, there would be an initial positive response followed by opposition from some hostile Jewish people, after which Paul would turn to preach to the Gentiles in the city, and then the crowds would be so stirred up in such opposition to him over his preaching to the Gentiles that he eventually would need to leave the city. However, not all parts of that pattern were consistently followed, for the physician Luke, the probable author of the books of Luke and Acts and constant companion of Paul, reported that at least at Cyprus (13:5), Berea (17:10-12), Athens (17:17) and Ephesus (18:18), Paul preached in the synagogues with no apparent opposition from the Jewish audience. The opposition that did come to Paul in Berea was not from Jews in that city, anyway, but from Jews who trailed after Paul from Thessalonica (17:13). Moreover, even the pattern of "to the Jews first" must in a few instances be qualified, for often Paul's audience in the synagogues was composed of Jews and Gentiles (Acts 13:16b, 26; 17:17; 18:4; also 20:21). Perhaps this same reality was present even in those cases where it was not noted, but rather inferred that his audience was made up of Jew and Gentile, for when it comes time for Luke to record what the response to Paul's teaching was, he almost always referred to both Jews and Gentiles as being among those who accepted his message (13:43; 14:1; 17:4, 12; 19:10, 17). Therefore, Paul's use of the synagogue did not mean he was exclusively interested in the Jewish people, for he repeatedly claimed that he was sent to both Jew and Gentile. Moreover, since no churches had been built as yet, Paul was left with the sole option of using the synagogue for his preaching.

To complicate the matter a bit more, often there were Gentiles in the synagogue who were known as "God-fearers:" Gentiles who believed in the God of Israel and were observant for at least portions of the Torah.[17] Even so, despite their observance of much that was in the Law, they were

---

17 See the observations of Shaye J. D. Cohen, "Crossing the Boundary and Becoming a Jew," *Harvard Theological Review* 82 (1989): 13-33.

still regarded by the Jewish people as non-Jews (Acts 10:1–2), as they should have been. It is no wonder, then, that the outcome of Paul's preaching in the synagogue always resulted in some Jews and some Gentiles coming to faith in Yeshua as their Messiah. Paul very seldom spoke to the Gentiles outside of the synagogues, though there were a few such occasions (for instance, in the crowd at Lystra, 14:14–17; in the Areopagus in Athens, 17:22–31).

PAUL—THE APOSTLE TO THE GENTILES AS WELL

Thus we conclude that Paul was indeed an apostle to the Gentiles, but he was just as much a teacher of the Jewish people in Israel. In all three versions of his Damascus Road experience, this same fact is confirmed in one way or another. For example, in Acts 9:1–19a, this wider commission for Paul to reach out to both groups was contained in the words of Ananias: Ananias declared that Paul had been chosen by God to be God's special instrument to bear His name "before the Gentiles, kings and the sons of Israel" (9:15). But it is also true that when Paul was asked to give an account of his activity from his missionary journeys in the churches at Antioch and Jerusalem, three times he focused on his work among the Gentiles (14:27; 15:12; 21:19). But if we limit our analysis of the ministry of Paul merely to his Gentile success, we would miss the balance that is elsewhere presented, for instance Paul's words before King Agrippa in Acts 26:22–23. There he echoed the call to be a "light to the Gentiles," for as God's servant, he brought "salvation to the ends of the earth" (Isa 42:7). Paul told King Agrippa that he was doing nothing less than what the prophets and Moses said would take place in the coming days as he too proclaimed light "both to our people and to the Gentiles" (Acts 26:22–23). Paul was indeed an apostle to the Gentiles, but he never missed a chance to minister to his own people of Israel as well.

THE UNFORTUNATE PARTING OF THE WAYS BEGINS

For most of Paul's ministry, he continued to preach the word of God by going first to many of the synagogues he encountered in city after city on his missionary tours, even while he also simultaneously established new groups of Jewish and Gentile believers in Yeshua. But an unfortunate parting of the ways seems to have begun to take place in Acts 19:8–9, which reads:

> Paul entered the synagogue and spoke boldly there [in Ephesus] for three months, arguing persuasively about the kingdom of God. But some of them became obstinate; they refused to believe and publicly maligned the Way. So Paul left them. He took the disciples with him and had discussion daily in the lecture hall of Tyrannus [instead].

Earlier, when Paul ministered in the Ephesian synagogue, he was received quite positively (18:19–20), for that seems to be why Paul continued there for three months of ministry (19:8). But after this positive experience of acceptance came a break in Paul's relationship with the Jewish leaders of that synagogue. Some non-believing Jews "publicly maligned the Way." What happened here must have been of quite a serious nature, for Paul had faced opposition elsewhere on previous occasions, by way of verbal attacks (13:45; 18:6a), as pagan authorities also had tried to isolate the Gentile audience from Paul, as did many of those in the Jewish leadership (17:6–9; 18:12–16). The secular authorities, however, must have usually regarded such outbreaks as minor disputes among the Jews, but the opposition of Jewish people from the synagogues, who understood more of what was at stake for them and for their future, took on a more serious obstacle to the preaching of the gospel. They wanted to separate the Jews in the synagogues from the Jewish believers in Yeshua.

As a result, the apostle Paul left the Ephesian synagogue and took his disciples (19:9) away with him. This would seem to be the first withdrawal of the Jewish believers from any synagogue and perhaps some of the first steps toward a separate new community of the Yeshua/Jesus believers.

NEW OPPOSITION FROM THE JERUSALEM JEWISH AUTHORITIES

The twelve disciples that were left, after Yeshua had ascended up to heaven, often faced harassment and some arrest from the temple authorities (Acts 4:1–3; 5:17–18). This period can be framed by the three times when serious action was taken against the Jerusalem believers: (1) the persecution that began with the martyrdom of Steven, in which Saul (renamed Paul) participated wholeheartedly as an opponent of "the Way" by holding the coats of those throwing the stones (Acts 8:1–3; 9:1–2); (2) the persecution in c. A.D. 42 instituted by King Herod Agrippa I (called only as "Herod" in Acts 12:1), where the apostle James, son of Zebedee, was executed (12:1-3); and (3) the third event in c. A.D. 62, when James, the brother of Yeshua, was martyred along with several others.[18] All three instances seem to be when the reigning high priest was one who belonged to the Saducean family[19] of Annas/Ananias, i.e., Caiaphas, son-in-law to Annas, who presided at the trial of Jesus, and who was still the high priest when Stephen was tried before the council. His son Matthias succeeded Annas in A.D. 43.

After James's death in A.D. 62, Hegesippus and the Jerusalem bishop's list, agree in naming Simeon, the son of Cleopas, and first cousin to Yeshua and James (half brother of Yeshua), as the successor to James in leading the Jerusalem Church.[20]

However, the outbreak of the Jewish revolt in Rome in A.D. 66 must have presented enormous difficulties for the Jews in Jerusalem, as it did for all Jewish Christians. By now the persons who followed "the Way" were too noticeable for them to merely abstain from expressing support to the revolutionary leaders, so, according to Eusebius,

> the people of the church in Jerusalem were commanded, according to an oracle given by revelation to trustworthy persons there before the war, to leave the city [of Jerusalem] and live in one of the cities of Perea, which they call Pella[21]

A good number appear to have done just that! (See our chapter on "Pella" in this book). This certainly seems possible, because the Jerusalem Church seems to have survived the war against the Jewish people, as the bishop's

---

18   Josephus. *Antiquities*, 20.199-203.

19   Richard Bauckham, "James and the Jerusalem Community," in *The Early Centuries: Jewish Believers in Jesus*, 75.

20   James emerged as a leader in the Jerusalem church (Acts 1:13; 12:2, 17; 15:13; 21:18).

21   Eusebius. *Hist. eccl.* 3.5.3.

list of Jewish Bishops indicates. After the momentous events of A.D. 70, these overseers of "the Way" continued leading what later became known as the "Christian church." Moreover, one of the main centers of the Jewish believers in Palestine in the second century was east of the Jordan (including Pella). This is not to deny, however, that there were any Jewish Christian communities that remained west of the Jordan after A.D. 70, for later Bar Kokhba will take action against many Christians still in Judea at the time of the second Jewish revolt against Rome in A.D. 132–135.[22]

THE EXILE OF THE NAZARENES FROM THE CHRISTIAN MOVEMENT

It would appear that a further rupture in the Jewish–Gentile relations occurred, then, after the second Jewish Revolt (A.D. 132–135) during the reign of Hadrian (A.D. 106–138). The Gentile believers could no longer support the national aspirations (of a revolt against Rome) of some of the "Nazarenes,"[23] for the destruction of Jerusalem in A.D. 133–135, and the false messianic claims of Bar-Kokhba, that he was the real Messiah (even though these false messianic claims were wrongfully and amazingly supported even by such an esteemed authority as Rabbi Akiba) were too much for the Gentile believers who believed that only Yeshua was the Messiah. This is not to say that all of the Nazarenes, or that all of the Pharisaic party, acknowledged Bar-Kokhba as the Messiah, for one of them quipped about their own Rabbi Akiba and his unbelievable support of Bar-Kokhba, "Akiba, grass will grow out of thy chin before Messiah come[s]."[24] In fact, Bar-Kokhba was known for his ruthlessness (e.g., he commanded his soldiers to cut off one of their fingers to prove their loyalty

---

22 See James J. Bloom, *The Jewish Revolts Against Rome, A.D. 66–135: A Military Analysis* (Jefferson: NC: McFarland, 2010), 209-16.

23 Nazoraeans was a term used for some of the early Jewish believers, who were ethnic Jews, who were believers in Yeshua and who still practiced a Jewish way of life. Some recognized the deity of Yeshua as the Messiah, but some did not recognize His divinity. This term could be an overarching term for two other sub-categories: the Ebionites and the Mimouni.

24 Lamentations Rabbah 2:5 & Jerusalem Talmud, Ta'anit 4:8 (cited in Alieza Salzberg, "Judaism after the Temple, http://www.myjewishlearning.com/article/judaism-after-the-temple/, last visited April 17, 2017).

to him and as evidence of their courage, just as he also ruthlessly executed his aged uncle Rabbi Eleazar of Modeim).[25] In this manner he also persecuted the Jewish Christians.

SUMMARY

There is no doubt that the early expressions of what was later called the "Christian movement" began largely first of all among the Jewish people, with the Gentile community of believers trailing further behind in numbers and leadership, and coming much later in time. But from those early days, the group was certainly mixed and had both Jews and Gentiles as believers in Yeshua as the Messiah, whose coming had been prophesied in the Tanach (Old Testament).

What greatly upset this basic harmony between the two groups was the revolt of A.D. 66–70, which was further damaged by the second revolt of A.D. 132–135, wherein a Jewish mortal named Bar Kokhba, "son of [the] star" presumed to claim full deity and Messiah-ship (based on the Num 24:17 prophecy about a coming "Star"). More than any other blockage, these two events were transformational for both the Jewish and Gentile audiences.

---

25 Alexander Zephyr, *Rabbi Akiva, Bar Kokhba Revolt, and the Ten Tribes of Israel* (Bloomington, IN: iUniverse LLC, 2013), 3-4.

CHAPTER 2

WHEN SUPERSESSIONISM AND REPLACEMENT THEOLOGY DREW UP LINES[26]

☙

Sculpted on either side of many early European cathedral portals are two attractive and usually young-looking female figures known in Latin as *Ecclesia et Synagoga*, meaning, of course, the "church and synagogue." They personify the Christian church and the Jewish synagogue, but usually in an antagonistic spirit. The most famous example is that on the Strasbourg Cathedral, but the same two figures can be found on the portals of other cathedrals such as Minden, Bamberg, Metz, Freiburg Minister, all those in Germany, with Notre Dame in Paris, as well as some vestiges of the same in some churches remaining after the destruction of the English Reformation on the cathedrals at Rochester, Salisbury, and Winchester in the United Kingdom.

These figures represent the hallmarks of what later became known as "supersessionism," or "replacement theology," the Christian belief that the church now "sat on [the seat]" (Latin, *super*, meaning "on," or "upon" and *sedere*, meaning "to sit") of promises God had previously given to Israel, but now had allegedly been given over to the Christian church. Thus the seat formerly occupied by Israel was now superseded by the Christian church due to the Jewish resolute disobedience to the law of God, and her

---

26 Hillsdale College Gershom Lectures, lecture 11, January 19–21, 2014 and Robert Cooley Lectures in Early Christianity at Gordon Conwell Theological Seminary in Charlotte, N.C. on January 15–16, 2015.

rejection of Yeshua as the long-awaited Messiah. As many in the Christian church assumed this seat, it only increased the rupture between the Jewish people and the Gentile believers. In keeping with this view of things, thus the figure of *Synagoga* was frequently pictured in the sculptured porticos as a blindfolded woman (perhaps a reference to Paul's statement about how many Jewish people were blinded from seeing what God had said in the Scripture, as noted in 2 Cor 3:13-16). Furthermore, *Synagoga* was also pictured with a drooping head that was looking down as she carried a broken lance (perhaps a possible allusion to the lance that was used to stab Christ), with the Tablets of the Torah scrolls (Law) beginning to slip out of her hands.

On the other side of the cathedral entrance, *Ecclesia* was usually presented as adorned with a crown and a chalice (perhaps for catching the blood coming from the side of our bleeding Lord and a symbol of the Eucharist), along with a cross-topped staff, as she looked out confidently toward the future.

These two sculpted figures on church portals were generally found in cathedrals in the larger cities of northern Europe, where a significant number of Jewish communities existed, especially in Germany. Along with their theological significance, these figures were to remind the Jewish community of their place in that society, implying, of course, a Jewish submission within the Gentile Christian realm. They now had to take an inferior position to those in the church, for they had failed to obey the Law, and they had killed Yeshua as well.

Since much ordinary business was conducted in those days in many of these cathedrals, many Jewish people would need to pass by the portals of these cathedrals with these figures staring them in the face as they came and went. In most of these earlier examples, there was perhaps no open hostility directly intended, but in the later examples, such as on the fifteenth-century Erfurt Cathedral, it depicts the same pair jousting on horses with *Ecclesia* apparently winning. The inference was clear: a separation had come between the synagogue and the church!

It was especially with the influx into Western Europe of the Jewish population in the late tenth- to the twelfth-century Renaissance, however, that an increasing contact resumed between Christian theologians and Jewish scholars. Such a contact made the Christians more aware of alternative ways of interpreting the Scriptures and therefore they were stimulated to counter this scholarship, or challenged by it to develop an opposing position, one in which the church emerged as the victor and the synagogue was seen as the loser. This helped to lay the grounds for a "Christian replacement theology" and a basic antagonism between the Jewish and Christian communities.

THE RISE OF A "CHRISTIAN REPLACEMENT THEOLOGY"

So how did a seemingly harmonious relationship between the Jewish Christian believers in Messiah and the Gentile followers of the "Way" in the first century, and into the second century, turn out to be so sour and eventually downright hostile? Was it not true that Yeshua was indeed Jewish? And had not the Bible been written by forty writers, thirty-nine of which were certainly Jewish? Even the writer Luke, Paul's personal companion and physician, was possibly the only non-Jewish writer of the 66 books of Scripture. But even he may have been a convert to Judaism as well.

None of the early followers of Yeshua thought they were starting a new religion, for they centered the gospel they taught squarely on the books and the message of the Tanach (Old Testament). When the early disciples and Church Fathers began to preach the gospel to others outside of Judah and Jerusalem, they always began the story of redemption with Abraham, Isaac, and Jacob, which message the apostle Paul declared was nothing less than the gospel itself (Gal 3:8). Therefore, the church later would view itself (as taught by revelation) as grafted into the olive tree, whose trunk was from Israel, and from which many of the natural Jewish branches had been temporarily lopped off until they returned back by faith into the trunk of that tree to which they belonged—a faith in Messiah (Rom 9–11).

Why, then, in the later centuries did such severe animosity break out between Jews and Gentiles that, such professed cities of Gentile Christianity, such as Rome, for example, would force Jews to wear a yellow insignia on their clothing and live in a Jewish ghetto? It was not until Napoleon's armies conquered Rome in A.D. 1809, and opened the gates of the ghetto, where the Jews were locked within these walls each night, that such evils would be temporarily undone. Thus, it took a Gentile conqueror named Napoleon to unlock the gates of the ghetto and grant the full rights of citizenship to these Jewish people. However, when Napoleon later suffered a series of defeats and the collapse of his regime in A.D. 1814, the Vatican regained control of Rome and its nearby territories,. Then Pope Pius VII forced the Jews back into their ghetto and reinstated all the prior restrictions against the Jews. As a result the harassment against the Jewish people continued!

But this anti-Jewish reaction by the Vatican in the early nineteenth century was not a new feature for the Jewish community; this was but the continuation of hostility towards the Jewish people that had been going on for a number of centuries. The Roman Catholic Church, unfortunately, was merely acting out what had begun to develop soon after the middle of the second Christian century, when the church had incorrectly taught that due to Israel's failure to believe or obey the covenant God gave them, they had been replaced by the church, which Gentile believers now sat in Israel's seat of privilege. The resulting action often logically led to reducing the Jews to a ghetto and even worse types of actions.

The split between the Jewish ethnic practice of the faith and that of the Gentile believers, then, must have begun to harden somewhere around the mid-second century. The most outspoken theologian of this period and for this cause was the Church Father Justin Martyr (c. 100–165), especially in his work entitled *Dialogue with Trypho* (c. A.D. 153). In this book, Justin debated with a learned Jewish scholar named Trypho, where in chapter 11 he made the point that will later become the celebrated cause of "replacement theology" for years to come. He argued:

> We [Christians] have been led to God through the crucified Christ, and we are the true spiritual Israel, and the descendants of Judah, Jacob, Isaac, and Abraham who, though uncircumcised, was approved and blessed by God because of his faith and was called the father of many nations.[27]

In Justin's dialogue number 44, he avers that the Jews are "sadly mistaken" if they think that just because they are descendants of the biblical

---

27 Justin Martyr, *Dialogue with Trypho*, dialogue 11 as cited by Jeffrey Siker, *Disinheriting the Jews* (Louisville, KY: Westminster/John Knox, 1991), 166-67.

patriarchs that they will share in the benefits of the legacy of God's promise. Justin expands on this claim in dialogue number 119:

> We Christians are not only a people, but a holy people ... nor just any nation... but the chosen people of God... For this is really the nation promised to Abraham by God when he told him He would make him the father of many nations ... And we [Christians] shall inherit the Holy Land together with Abraham, receiving our inheritance for all eternity, because by our similar faith we have become children of Abraham.... Thus, God promised Abraham a religious and righteous nation of like faith, and a delight to the Father; but it is not you [Jews to whom it is given] "in whom there is no faith."[28]

Justin incorrectly felt that Israel had been totally dispossessed of her promises in the Abrahamic and Davidic Covenants. Therefore, what had been promised to Israel, including the land of Canaan, would now belong to the Church. This seems to mark the beginning of supersessionism and replacement theology in Christianity. It would develop the seeds of anti-Semitism and sprout in the awful days of the German Holocaust/*Shoah*.

Just as significant was the act whereby the Emperor Constantine gathered all the bishops of the church in the thirtieth year of his reign, which he viewed as a foreshadowing of the eschatological messianic banquet spoken of in Scripture. For Constantine, there was no need to distinguish between the church and the empire, for together they fulfilled God's kingdom on earth. Constantine had made the new faith in Jesus Christ, which he had found in his own conversion, the official and legal religion of the empire he controlled.

At the Council of Nicea in A.D. 325, Constantine declared that the Christian celebration of Easter should no longer be linked to the Jewish Passover, for, as he put it, "It is unbecoming that on the holiest of festivals, we should follow the customs of the Jews; henceforth let us have nothing

---

28 Siker, *Disinheriting the Jews*, 13, 175.

in common with this odious people."²⁹ Constantine also made it a crime for the Jews to proselytize persons to the Jewish faith.

Later in that same fourth century, a man named Augustine was baptized outside of Rome in A.D. 387. Augustine later was to embrace a replacement theology, since he felt that God had cast off the house of Israel. Because of his prolific writing and his esteem among believers, then and now, his views on a displaced, disowned Israel, which was replaced by the church, have become almost official church doctrine now for a millennium and three quarters for many church confessions, especially in Roman Catholic and for many in the Protestant Reformed theology.

But even more damaging to Jewish–Christian relations was the series of anti-Jewish sermons given by the bishop of Antioch, John Chrysostom, in that s2ame year of A.D. 387, when Augustine was baptized. Whereas Justin Martyr and Augustine had been somewhat milder in their attack on the Jews, Chrysostom's rhetoric knew few boundaries as he stressed the Jewish "deicide" of Yeshua as the ultimate Jewish crime. "Deicide" was simply this: the Jews "killed God" when they crucified Yeshua! Since Israel had shed the precious blood of Christ, there could no longer be any restoration, any pardon or any mercy for them: Chrysostom called for a bloody retribution on the Jewish people. Thus, the connection between the replacement of Israel with the church and the call for the elimination of the Jewish people was now made complete. Chrysostom's rhetoric was altogether out of control, as he preached this message of hate at the close of the fourth Christian century. Now synagogues would be attacked and burnt to the ground, resulting in the fact that often they would later be replaced on the very same premises by a Christian church. It is little wonder that the symbol of the Christian cross would be so revolting a symbol to most Jewish people.

The first recorded case of an attack on a synagogue was in northern Italy led by Bishop Innocentius of Dertona, who died in A.D. 355. Christians repeated a similar act in Tipasa, in North Africa, and again some thirty years later in Rome. In the east, a monk named Barsauma (c. A.D. 400) with forty other monks destroyed several synagogues and

---

29   Cited in David Brog, *Standing with Israel: Why Christians Support the Jewish State* (Lake Mary, FL: Front Line, 2006), 26.

consecrated the remains of these synagogues as churches. The false doctrinal views of the Christian church were clearly responsible for all of this anti-Jewish violence. What Chrysostom had started had now led from a replacement theology, as reinforced at the Council of Nicea in A.D. 325, all the way up to the Council at Basel in 1434[30] with a sorry string of acts of infamy against the Jewish people encouraged. The litany of these key tragic steps may be traced as follows (or even one begun in A.D. 306 before Nicea):

> Synod of Elvia (306)—intermarriage, sexual intercourse and sharing of meals between Christians and Jews were all prohibited.
>
> Synod of Clermont (535)—Jews were not to hold public office.
>
> Synod of Orleans (538)—Jews could not own Christian slaves or employ Christian servants.
>
> Synod of Gerona (1078)—Jews must pay taxes to support the church to the same extent as Christians.
>
> Third Lateran Council (1179)—Jews may not sue or be a witness against Christians in the courts.
>
> Fourth Lateran Council (1215)—Jews are required to wear a distinctive dress (eventually implemented by a yellow badge).
>
> Council of Oxford (1222)—New synagogues may not be built.
>
> Synod of Breslau (1267)—Jews must live in ghettos.
>
> Synod of Ofen (1279)—Christians may not sell or rent real estate to Jews.
>
> Council of Basel (1434)—Jews may not obtain academic degrees.

The list is enough to cause a huge outcry to the God of heaven: how could He have allowed this to continue with little or no reprieve from the Christians and society?

---

30 This list is a slightly modified list found in Brog, *Standing with Israel*, 27.

THE JEWISH PEOPLE DURING THE REFORMATION

Later the Protestant Reformation grew out of Martin Luther's nailing his 95 theses to the door of the Wittenburg Church in the early 1500s. As a result, the long-term hold that the Roman Catholic Church had on the church in the west was about to be broken. This break with the Roman church, however, provided a golden opportunity for newly formed Protestant churches to open a new door to the Jewish people, who up to this point had suffered so much from so many Gentile nations. Yet, instead of Luther and the reformers challenging the Roman church's position on their relations with the Jewish people, along with Luther they embraced replacement theology, even after Luther had been initially favorably disposed to the possibility of Jewish conversions to faith in Yeshua. What is more, he took the replacement idea even further in his radical rhetoric of anti-Jewish violence. In one of his later works, entitled *The Jews and Their Lies*, Luther set forth his own program of dealing with the Jews, which in some cases led directly to some of the rhetoric used as the bases for Adolph Hitler's own rhetoric and the awful acts that resulted in the Holocaust, or *Shoah*, and the murder of some six million Jewish people! Luther's speech was inflammatory, to say the least, for he ordered:

> First, their synagogues or churches should be set on fire, and whatever does not burn up should be covered or spread over with dirt so that no one may ever be able to see a cinder or stone of it. And this ought to be done for the honor of God and Christianity in order that God may see that we are Christians .... Secondly, their homes should be broken down and destroyed. Thirdly, they should be deprived of their prayer books and Talmuds in which such idolatry, lies, and blasphemy are taught.

> Fourthly their Rabbis must be forbidden under threat of death to teach any more .... Fifthly, passport and traveling privileges should be absolutely forbidden the Jews. Let them stay at home. Sixthly, they ought to be stopped from usury. As said before, everything they possess they stole and robbed from us through their usury, for they have no other means of support.

Seventhly, let the young and strong Jews and Jewesses be given the flail, the ax, the hoe, the spade, the distaff and spindle, and let them earn their bread by the sweat of their noses as is enjoined upon Adam's children.

If, however, we are afraid that they might harm us personally, or our wives, children, servants, cattle, etc., then let us apply the same cleverness as the other nations such as France, Spain, Bohemia, etc., and settle with them for which they have extorted from us, after having it divided up fairly, let us drive them out of the country for all time. [31]

Accordingly, for the believer who espoused Reformed convictions, often there was a strong tendency to continue the Augustinian theology of an exclusion of the Jewish people from the ancient promises that God had made with the Jewish patriarchs, but were now made over the Christian church, which was being referred to as the "new Israel."

Nevertheless, there were some examples of a more pro-Judaic stance. For example, the European Wilhelmus a Brakel (1635–1711), a well-known Dutch Reformed theologian in Rotterdam, Holland, took issue with the standard ancient Augustinian line of interpreting these Scriptures about the promise made to Israel by God. Brakel held that the church was not to be identified with the term the "New Israel," but Paul was referring to a real ethnic Jewish people when he wrote that "all Israel would be saved" (Rom 11:25). Moreover, he held that the Jews would return to their land, for the promise here was not about the eternal rest in heaven, but about the land of Canaan.[32]

One must not overlook the amazing contribution of the Puritans to the development of Judeo-Christian tradition. [33] The Puritans were a

---

31 As cited by Brog, *Standing with Israel*, 28-29 from the *Encyclopedia Judaica* and John Hagee, *Should Christians Support Israel?* (San Antonio, TX: Dominion Publishers, 1987), 18-19.

32 As argued by Wilhelm VanGemeren, "Israel as the Hermeneutical Crux in the Interpretation of Prophecy," *Westminster Theological Journal* 45 (1983): 142-43.

33 I am grateful for Daniel Juster calling to my attention this development, especially in his work, *Passion for Israel: A Short History of the Evangelical Church's Commitment to the Jewish People and Israel* (Clarksville, MD: Lederer Books, 2012), Chapter 1.

movement within the English, and later in the American Church, whose history could be seen from the accession of Elizabeth I in 1559 to the restoration of Charles II in 1660. Not all Puritans were agreed on an agenda, for there were those who were concerned about the compromises in Anglicanism that allowed unqualified clergy to serve. This was regarded as a wrong type of conformity in doctrine and practice, one that was too Roman Catholic for the tastes of some. Some wanted to stay with the Church of England and others wanted to reform the church to be a Scottish Presbyterian type of Church. Another group of Puritans, known as the Separatists, were the ones who came to Plymouth, Massachusetts in 1620 on the *Mayflower*.

Puritans were committed to Bible study and to a straightforward reading of the text. Therefore, they took the divine promises made to Abraham, Isaac, and Jacob as being straightforward and literal, and so they looked forward to the preservation of the Jewish people in the end time. Thomas Brightman (1562–1607) was the first to write on the Jewish restoration. He was followed by Giles Fletcher and Thomas Draxe and Sir Henry Finch. These writers focused on Romans 11, which provided for a grafting in of the Gentile believes into the olive tree trunk of Israel, but there would come a day when all Israel would be saved in the end times, wherein the Jewish people who believed in Yeshua would themselves be reattached to the olive tree by faith. Thus the seventeenth-century Puritans were adamant in their defense of the chosen-ness of Israel as Samuel Rutherford's book, *Lex Rex*, demonstrates.

Elnathan Parr contributed to this same line of thought by writing his commentary on Romans, where he argued against a Christian replacement of Israel, but he did it in most winsome ways. Others added to the argument in favor of the Jewish people, such as John Milton in his *Paradise Regained*.

As a result of this flourish of writing activity, the Puritan views in favor of the Jews led to Cromwell's inviting the Jewish people back to England after Richard the Lionhearted had expelled them in the thirteenth century.

By the time the seventeenth century arrived, Lutheranism had so cooled in its doctrinal orthodoxy, which had given rise to a godly reform movement of the Pietistic emphasis of Philipp Jacob Speener (1635–1705) of Frankfurt and Berlin and August Hermann Francke (1663–1727) of Leipzig. At the University of Halle they developed a greater tolerance for the Jewish people. There followed a long line of Lutheran scholars, such as Bengel, Zahn, (Franz) Delitzsch, Godet and the American Lutherans named Joseph Seiss and George N. H. Peters, who developed a premillennial theology that was friendly to the Jewish cause, their return to their land, and their future salvation in the end day, thereby toning down some of the shrill emphases of Luther.

Another strong movement that paralleled the Pietist movement was the Moravian Movement, started by Count Nicholas Ludwig von Zinzendorf (1700–1760). He was raised by Pietist mother and educated at the University of Halle, where he was under the teaching of A. Francke. By 1722, Zinzendorf, who had taken over the responsibilities for his family's Saxon estate, opened up an area of the estate for the persecuted remnant of the Hussite Movement in Moravia, made up of the Bohemian Brethren, who named the village they established as "Herrnhut." They too were sympathetic to the promises given to Israel.

THE DEVELOPMENT OF REFORMED THEOLOGY [34]

Much of what became known as Reformed Theology was grounded in the earlier Augustinian doctrine in which the church replaced Israel, especially as it involved their views on eschatology. A classic example of this emphasis could be found in the writings of Francis Turretin (1623–1687), for he also studied at Calvin's academy in Geneva, where he later taught for thirty years. His elenctic theology became the hallmark of Reformed doctrine in the next centuries, as he quoted Augustine copiously, and it continued to be used on into the nineteenth century, especially by the early theologians of Princeton Theological Seminary.

For example, Turretin argued that before the end of this age, there would be an enormous conversion of the Jews and incorporation into the church (exclusive of their continuing any Jewish identity), but as for

---

34 I am indebted to Barry E. Horner, *Future Israel: Why Christian Anti-Judaism Must Be Challenged* (Nashville, TN: B & H), 2007, 159-78 for the discussion in this section.

any further prophetic expectations for Israel beyond their return from Babylon, Turretin had this to say:

> The expressions [about Israel's return to the land in the end days] are not to be pressed literally, because they are symbolical, not proper; typical not literal; to be explained spiritually and not carnally. Israel is to be restored, not according to the flesh and letter, but according to the promise and spirit (Rom 9); the holy city, not Jerusalem, but the Church.[35]

In the nineteenth and twentieth centuries, a "new hermeneutic" arose, which actually was a slightly revised Augustinianism, which came as a response to a resurgence of the pre-millennialism that had first appeared, and which had held the dominate position originally in the church for the first three or four Christian centuries, but was now experiencing a comeback in such Lutherans as Johann A. Bengel (1687–1752), Theodor Zahn (1838–1933), Franz Delitzsch (1813–1890), and Frederic L. Godet (1812–1900) along with the American Lutherans named George N. H. Peters (1825–1909), Joseph A. Seiss (1823–1904) and especially Samuel Simon Schmucker.

On the other hand, among the leaders of the a-millennial position were Patrick Fairbairn (1805–1874), Herman Bavinck (1895–1964) and Gerhardus Vos (1862–1949). Fairbairn's views, in particular, are hard to pin down, for in 1838–39 he delivered twelve lectures in which he made the case for a-millennial eschatology, having first being pre-millennial, with a distinct national return of Israel to their land, and a conversion of the Jewish people. But then by 1864, a now older Fairbairn, who had by now become Principal of the Presbyterian Free Church College in Glasgow, Scotland, authored the book *Fairbairn on Prophecy*, which took an a-millennial position that adopted essentially an Augustinian view.

No less affirming of the same Augustinian view was Herman Bavinck, who was born in Hoogeveen, Netherlands in 1854. He attended the theological School in Kampen, and then he moved to Leiden, where in graduated in 1880 by completing a dissertation on Ulrich Zwingli. In 1882 he

---

35 Francis Turretin. *Institutes of Elenctic Theology* (Phillipsburg, NJ: P & R, 1992–94), 2:163.

began to teach theology for a time for the Christian Reformed churches and in 1902 he joined the faculty of Free University of Amsterdam as Professor of Systematic Theology. In his view:

> The spiritualization of the Old Testament, rightly understood, is not an invention of Christian theology but has its beginnings in the New Testament itself. The Old Testament in spiritualized form, that is, the Old Testament stripped of its temporal and sensuous form, is the New Testament....All Old Testament concepts shed their external, national-Israelitish meanings and become manifest in their spiritual and eternal sense.[36]

Bavinck goes on to identify who the true children of Abraham really are: they are those who believe in Christ, not the Jews who reject Christ (Rom 2:28–29). Thus, this new community of believers replaced carnal, national Israel in all aspects. Bavinck was a supercessionist in every sense of the word.

No less significant, if not more so, was Geerhardus Vos, who had a profound influence on a number of other Reformed writers. Though he was born at Friesland, Netherlands in 1862, he was raised in a Christian Reformed manse in Michigan, where he began his theological studies in the denominational school in Grand Rapids, but later continued those studies in Princeton Seminary, Berlin, and Strassburg. He returned to the states and taught at first in Grand Rapids, but then became Professor of Biblical Theology in 1893 at Princeton until he retired in 1932. Even though Vos vehemently opposed any type of premillennialism (or "chiliasm"), yet because of his exegesis of Zechariah 12 and Romans 11, he felt forced to acknowledge a future conversion of Israel. However, Vos was careful not to discuss whether such a "mass conversion" was connected to a national future restoration to the land of Israel, for he correctly knew had he done so he would have crossed the line and entered millennial territory. [37]

---

36 Herman Bavinck, *The Last Things* (Grand Rapids: Baker, 2000), 96-97.

37 Horner, *Future Israel*, 175.

AN ERRONEOUS CHRISTOCENTRIC REINTERPRETATION OF THE OLD TESTAMENT

In recent years, a new hermeneutical principle has appeared that imposes the New Testament revelation of Yeshua on the Old Testament in such a way that the new covenant becomes the dominate interpretive tool over the Old Testament by *reinterpreting* the entirety of that testament Christologically. Anglican representatives from the United Kingdom of such an anti-Judaic methodology include Colin Chapman, Steve Motyer, Stephen Sizer, Peter Walker and N. T. Wright. The American examples of the same approach to Scripture would be Anthony Hoekema, William Hendriksen, Hans K. LaRondelle and O. Palmer Robertson.

Barry Horner singled out George Eldon Ladd of Fuller Seminary, whom he felt is often incorrectly labeled as the premiere "Historic Pre-millennialist." Instead, however, he is among those who advocated this Christocentric *reinterpretation* of the Old Testament prophecies, by reading the New Testament back into the Old Testament. In Ladd's view there was only one passage that argued for a pre-millennial position in Scripture—Revelation 20; the Old Testament gave no evidence whatsoever for any type of chiliasm. Thus he identified more with the Augustinian position than that advocated by other nineteenth-century pre-millennial writers such as Joseph A. Seiss, David Baron, Adolph Safir, B. W. Newton, H. Grattan Guinness, J. C. Ryle, Charles Haddon Spurgeon, George Peters, Nathaniel West and Horatius Bonar.

Ladd affirmed that:

> Old Testament prophecies must be interpreted in the light of the New Testament to find their deeper meaning. ... I do not see how it is possible to avoid the conclusion that the New Testament applies Old Testament prophecies to the New Testament church and in doing so identifies the church as spiritual Israel.[38]

---

38 George E. Ladd, "Historic Premillennialism," in *The Meaning of the Millennium*, ed. R. G. Clouse (Downers Grove, IL: InterVarsity, 1977), 23.

But surely such a hermeneutic of reinterpretation and transference of the meaning from the New Testament to the Old is an illegitimate method of interpreting Scripture, for it nullifies the literal, straightforward interpretation of the Old Testament passage and seems to leave no message for the Old Testament reader. Thus, the tendency of the Gentile church was to draw even further lines of separation between the Jewish roots of the believing community and the Christian church.

THE HOLOCAUST/*SHOAH*[39]

There can be little doubt that centuries of Christian anti-Semitism unfortunately prepared Europe to readily accept and permit Nazi anti-Semitism. Nazism, with the apparent blessing of the church, became but a new name for the already rampant anti-Semitism that had been spawned in the heart of the Christian church. None of the Nazis were ever excommunicated from their churches, including Adolph Hitler himself. In fact, it is hard to explain how Nazism could have flourished so quickly and spread so extensively in Europe had it not been for the fact that the way for its appearance had been so deeply ingrained for centuries into the hearts and minds of so many by Christian replacement theology and supersessionism in the church.

As the Nazis came to power in 1933, they began passing a series of laws that forced the Jews into a separate existence. The laws of the Third Reich in almost every case were based on precedents that had been previously incorporated into church law.

On July 8, 1933, the Vatican signed a Concordat with Hitler, which became the Roman Catholic Church's first bilateral treaty with a foreign power. In that treaty, the Vatican promised to remove the Catholic church from any type of political opposition against Hitler's regime. Thus, when the Nazis moved into Rome to take away Rome's Jews on October 16, 1943, the Jews were herded into the central square of the Jewish Ghetto and on October 18 they boarded a train headed for Auschwitz. As the train left the station, Allied aircraft attacked the train, but the attempt to halt it failed. During the five-day trip in cattle cars, the Jews begged

---

39   *Shoah* is the Hebrew word for the Holocaust.

for water, but there was no sympathy extended, for when that five-day train ride was over, nearly all 1000 passengers would be gassed to death at Auschwitz, except 196 admitted to the work camp (of which only fifteen survived the war). The pope made no formal or public statement, either about the Jewish roundup or their deportation. Only after their deaths did he give a rather general statement lamenting "the suffering of all innocents" and the "suffering of so many unfortunate people," [40] but never mentioning the Jews by name.

SUMMARY

It is to be deeply regretted that the whole Jewish–Christian alliance around Yeshua the Messiah fell apart so early in the early history of the Church. What is even more tragic is the fact that the church's anti-Semitism and its replacement theology created an even deeper divide between the two factions that it is well-nigh to impossible to bridge, even up to this present day, except for the grace of God, or to expect any type of rapprochement or fellowship centered around a love for Messiah and a love for each other. Supersessionism and replacement theology have worked an evil that has practically eliminated a whole group of people from experiencing the gracious benefits of the death and resurrection of Yeshua. The fact that some of this will be rectified in the second appearance of Yeshua when "all Israel will be saved" will hardly excuse many in the Christian church for its complicity in the worldwide movement of anti-Semitism. There are enormous grounds for a time of confession by the Christian church and a request for forgiveness on behalf of both parties, but it would seem that the church should take the lead due to its active anti-Semitic role over the centuries. May God grant his grace to both parties so that a reuniting around Yeshua the Messiah might be possible once again.

---

40 As cited by Brog, *Standing with Israel*, 33.

CHAPTER 3

WHEN THE CHRISTIAN CHURCH NEEDS ISRAEL AND ISRAEL NEEDS THE CHURCH[41]

Had Yahweh not called and chosen the people of Israel to be His means of blessing all the nations on the face of the earth, the nation of Israel might never have been noticed, or figured so prominently in the world of human events, much less in the all-encompassing program and plan of God. However, it is also true that without the Jewish Scriptures, which came from the mouth of God through the Jewish people, and the promises to the patriarchs forming the roots of that divine plan, there would have been no salvation for humanity either. The Jewish people originally had constituted the very trunk of the olive tree that the apostle Paul talked about in Romans 11, into which the believing body of Gentile, as well as Jewish, believers were later grafted. And had that same trunk not been available as the anchor for all the believing community, the church would merely have floated in space without any firm hold on to reality, or without any tying of the church to anything in historical space and time; the church would be without a past and without a covenant that would tie its past and present into any future hope or in the plan of God as well.

But what, then, is the current connection between the Jewish people and the rise of the Christian church in the Christian centuries? Must the church, as it were, reinvent itself, by giving itself an alternate

---

41 From the Gershom Lectures in Judaism and Jewish Christian Relationships, Hillside College, January 19–21, 2014.

reinterpretation of the Old Testament Scriptures read back from the New Testament, and then haughtily assert its presence by sitting in the seat originally designated to be a promise to Israel? What has happened to the divine promises that were originally reserved for Israel? Surely, if the Church has taken away Israel's promises, that would be a way of raising a serious amount of hostility and animosity between the Jewish people and Christendom since they had been given originally to Israel by a God who cannot lie. Could these promises have been co-opted by the church? That view, usually referred to as "replacement theology" or "supersessionism," deserves a careful and studied long look once more. In fact, one would think that for some time now, the situation has called for both parties to work together in order to see just what went wrong after it all had started out to be a much more pleasant working climate—back when Jewish and Gentile believers used to be one.

AN EXAMINATION OF A CHRISTOCENTRIC REINTERPRETATION OF THE OLD TESTAMENT

However, despite this deep need for both parties to work together and to share in the same covenantal relationship, a Christian anti-Judaic attitude and a reworked eschatology for Israel may have been the source of much of the original divide between Jews and Gentiles to expect any type of joint worship and fellowship among believers from both sides of this debate. Some Christian interpreters may have meant this new spiritualized and allegorized reinterpretation of Old Testament Scriptures, allegedly from the New Testament, would be the best way for Christians to utilize the older testament. Nevertheless, this method of revising the interpretation of the Old Testament by employing the New Testament in re-explaining the older testament has brought about a "Christianizing" of the message of God that He gave in the older testament to the Jewish people, as well as to the nations at large. Often this has resulted in a process of evacuating the distinct and particular teaching found in the Old Testament by spiritualizing or allegorizing it into a symbolic and presumably a more spiritual word that is now offered to the church instead of to Israel.

Few interpreters today are currently as popular as the United Kingdom scholar N. T. Wright. The effect of his writing, unfortunately, has been one which erases the national as well as the land promises originally given to Israel, and in typical Augustinian fashion, these same promises are now made over instead to the church. N. T. Wright writes:

> He [Jesus] had not come to rehabilitate the symbol of the holy land, but to subsume it within a different fulfillment of the kingdom, which would embrace the whole creation. …. Jesus spent his whole ministry *redefining* what the kingdom meant. He refused to give up the symbolic language of the kingdom, but filled it with such new content that, …. he powerfully subverted [it from the] Jewish expectations.[42]

> Those who now belonged to Jesus' people were not identical with ethnic Israel, since Israel's history had reached its intended fulfillment; they claimed to be a continuation of Israel in a new situation… to fulfill Israel's vocation on behalf of the world.[43]

Instead of demonstrating how Israel and the Church needed each other, we are presented with the standard offensive line to Jewish people of the doctrine of supersessionism, only here N. T. Wright has put the same teaching clothed in a set of more moderate words. Rather than understanding the promises of God in the Old Testament as distinctive predictions of a future restoration of national or ethnic Israel about her land, and a coming genuine enormous repentance of the Jewish people on a huge scale, the promises of God to the Jewish people are merely "subsumed" within the kingdom of God, thereby showing that these promises should not be taken seriously, as if they would enjoy a literal, future fulfillment, or have a reality of their own in space and time.

Colin Chapman illustrated this same type of "spiritualizing" and reinterpreting of the Old Testament prophecies. He disappointingly argued:

> Christians today do not have the liberty to interpret the Old Testament in any way that appeals to them. Everything in the Old Testament has to be read through the eyes of the apostles.

---

42 N. T. Wright, *Jesus and the Victory of God* (London: SPCK, 1996), 446, 471

43 N.T. Wright, *The New Testament and the People of God* (London: ASCK, 1992), 457-58.

It is they who, so to speak, who give us the right spectacles for a genuinely Christian reading of the Old Testament. Therefore if Christians today find that certain details in books like Ezekiel appear to fit certain situations in the Middle East today, they should resist the temptation to draw direct connections with these contemporary events. The reason is that since the apostle John has given *his* interpretation of Ezekiel's visions, this should be seen as *the normative Christian interpretation* of these visions, and not only *one possible interpretation*.[44]

Here again, a strong Christian reinterpretation of the Old Testament texts is allowed to trump the plain and straightforward sense or reading of the older testament. But in order to do this, Chapman, along with N. T. Wright, and many others like them, must appeal somehow to the same Jewish Jesus and Jewish apostles to impose a new norm for reinterpreting and understanding the text of the older testament in a new Gentile way! Now there is an irony if I ever saw one!

Barry Horner, however, illustrated this improper hermeneutical move by citing a quotation from Steve Motyer, where Steve announced:

> Throughout the New Testament, we see the first Christians wrestling with the relationship between the "new" thing God has now done in Christ, and the "old" thing which he had done in Israel, and re-interpreting the latter in the light of the former. If we are to be New Testament Christians, we must do the same.... The New Testament "re-reading" of the Old Testament promises sees their climax in Jesus, and makes him the "end" of the story. The interpretation of the Old Testament prophecy and other "Israel" texts must be approached from the perspective of this basic New Testament teaching, and must follow the guidelines of New Testament interpretation .... The New Testament writers are "normative" for us, in showing us how to [re-]interpret Old Testament prophecy.[45]

---

44 Colin Chapman, *Whose Promised Land?* (Grand Rapids: Baker, 2002), 172. Emphasis his.

45 Horner, *Future Israel*, 189 from Steve Motyer, "Israel in God's Plan," *Evangelical Alliance Consultation*, June 2003. Special quotation marks are his.

But all this talk about a New Testament "reinterpretation" of the Old Testament overlooks how many times the Old Testament promises were rendered in a plain, obvious, natural, or straightforward sense! The idea that any and all moves from the earlier testament to the later testament involved moving from Old Testament "shadow" to New Testament "reality" forgets the long list of literally fulfilled prophecies found in the Old Testament. Take for instance the work of Horatius Bonar (1808–1889), better known as a beloved nineteenth-century hymn writer. On this subject of how directly we may be permitted to take the Old Testament prophecies made about Christ, Bonar has made quite a case for reading a good number of them in natural or literal way. He has given us an excellent example of what he meant by pointing to some of the messianic events in the Old Testament, which were fulfilled in as plain and literal a way as language [and subsequent history] could cite them and show their fulfillment. Bonar argued:

> In so far as prophecy has been already fulfilled, that fulfillment has [overwhelmingly] been a literal one. Take [for example] the predictions regarding the Messiah:
>
> His being born of the house of David;
>
> Of a virgin;
>
> At Bethlehem;
>
> Being carried down to and brought up out of Egypt;
>
> His healing diseases;
>
> His entering Jerusalem on an ass;
>
> His being betrayed by one of His disciples;
>
> His being left by all His familiar friends;
>
> His being smitten, buffeted and spit upon;
>
> His side being pierced;
>
> His bones unbroken;

His raiment divided by lot;

His receiving vinegar;

His being crucified between two thieves;

His being buried by a rich man;

His lying three days in a tomb;

His rising on the third day;

His ascending on high, and sitting at the right hand of God;

Bonar continued:

These and many other [Old Testament prophecies], have all been fulfilled to the very letter; far more literally than we could have ever conceived. And are not these fulfillments strong arguments in favor of the literality of all that yet remains behind? Nay, do they not furnish us with a distinct, unambiguous, and inspired canon of interpretation? [46]

This line of argumentation is so important to Jews and Christians rejoining their conversations and worshiping together again that it must be pursued further. God never intended that the two testaments should result in two separate religions: Judaism and Christianity. The Tanach (= OT) was meant to lead directly into the so-called New Testament and thus be the continuation of one plan from creation to consummation. When the divine promise-plan of God is ruptured and divided into two distinct parts, with the climax triumphing over the earlier revelation, then we have introduced a division where God had revealed the fulfillment of what he had revealed in earlier texts! Therefore, we must investigate further how this disparity appeared among the people of God.

---

[46] Horatius Bonar, *Prophetical Landmarks, Containing Data for Helping to Determine the Question of Christ's Premillennial Advent* (1847), 246-47. (It went through five editions). The forming of these fulfillments in a list is due to my arrangement and not that of Bonar.

ROADBLOCKS TO RETURNING TO THE ORIGINAL JEWISH–CHRISTIAN SYNTHESIS

From what we have outlined so far, it is clear that there must be a paradigm shift in the way many Christians thought about (and still do think about) the Jewish people and Israel if any peace, or any kind of rapprochement, is to come between Judaism and Christendom resulting in the eternal salvation of many Jewish people. Moreover, it is widely believed by most Christians that when the Jewish temple in Jerusalem was destroyed by the Romans in A.D. 70, it was because the Jewish people had failed to believe in Yeshua. This, then, resulted in the view that the destruction of the temple seemed to be a crisis for Judaism, for now they were without a center of worship, without priest, without sacrifice and still without a king. Some then thought that Christendom would now replace the temple along with the temple service in the institution of the church and thus become the New Israel that would now sit in the seat that had originally been occupied by Israel. Moreover, the New Covenant of Jeremiah 31:31–34 would now replace the Sinaitic Covenant, originally made between God and Israel. Thus, it was incorrectly argued that this New Covenant would antiquate the one made at Sinai and would bring it close to extinction—*at least this was according to the view of replacement theology*! Even in Judaism there appeared to be a type of replacement of sorts going on, for three things would replace the service of sacrifice of animals and the work of the high priest. These three replacements formed the three pillars of Judaism: repentance (Hebrew, *teshuvah*, "turning"), prayer (Hebrew, *tefilah*) and charity (Hebrew, *tsedakah*).

SIGNS OF DENOUNCING AN ANTI-JUDAISM IN SOME CHRISTIAN CHURCHES

However, there were some positive signs on the horizon. For example, since the time of St. Augustine, the a-millennial doctrine of the supersession of the church over national Israel was held by the Roman Catholic Church and often in some of the Reformed congregations. This view had been accorded the dominant conclusion since the fourth Christian century as held by many of these groups. However, at Vatican II the Roman Catholic Church released a papal bull entitled, *Nostra Aetate*, which read:

The Church, mindful of the patrimony she shares with the Jews and moved not by political reasons but by the Gospel's spiritual love, decries hatred, persecution, displays of anti-Semitism, directed against Jews at any time and by anyone.

However, despite this break-through, for which we can all be grateful, the interpretation of passages such as Ezekiel 36–37, Zechariah 14 and Romans 11 continued to be viewed in an allegorical or spiritual way as the impact of fourth-century Augustinianism remained, especially among many Reformed and Roman Catholic churches. However, Chiliasm, or pre-millennialism, as it was earlier understood, and as it dominated the first three Christian centuries of the church, , was regarded by these groups as a view that was usually associated with certain extreme forms of Anabaptist groups, or as a view that was exclusively linked with twentieth and twenty-first century form of classic Dispensationalism and historic pre-millennialism.

But the exegetical issues tended to remain where they have been for centuries. The question that always seemed to take pride of place was this: Was the Abrahamic Covenant a conditional or an unconditional covenant? Did it depend on the descendants of Abraham being faithful to the Lord and obeying the covenant, or was its continuance solely linked to the grace and mercy of God? That question was followed by another: If Abraham's Covenant remained in force, despite how Israel acted in the future, how did the covenant with David, or even the New Covenant figure into this plan if the Abrahamic Covenant continued in force? Was it true that the New Covenant was made with Israel and not with the New Testament church and that it therefore replaced the Sinaitic Covenant?

The answer to those questions can be stated in clear exegetical terms. The Abrahamic Covenant, first of all, rested on the faithfulness of Yahweh to his word, and it was not affected in its basic provisions, or in its continuance, by the happenstances of Israel, good or bad. In Genesis 15, it was Yahweh Himself, not Abraham, who walked between the divided pieces of the animal that were used to "make/cut [this] covenant" and who took the oath on His life that He would keep the terms of this covenant. Had Abraham been required to walk between the pieces, the covenant would have been constituted as a bilateral covenant, meaning that if either Abraham [including his descendants] or Yahweh failed to keep the provisions of the covenant, the terms of the covenant would be broken, and so the benefits would be discontinued. However, since only Yahweh put His life on the line, by walking between the pieces in Genesis 15, saying in effect, "May I, God, die, like these slain animals on either side of this aisle, if I do not keep my word," this was a unilateral covenant in which only God obligated Himself to maintain its promises.

Repeatedly through the older testament, God came to the rescue of Israel, even after they had fallen short of what He looked for in their lives. True, some in Israel never did enjoy the benefits of the promises of God, even though they have been required to transmit these same benefits to a later generation—as those in the line of David's kingship illustrated, for example. Thus, *transmission* of the promise of God was one thing, but *participation* in the benefits of that promise was an altogether different matter! But in Genesis 17, the covenant is mentioned thirteen times, making it the dominant concept of the chapter. But that chapter also repeatedly declares that this covenant is "everlasting" and "eternal" as well, mentioned about five times. Since God is also described as being "eternal" by the same word, it seems fair to say that the terms of this promise will be as enduring and lasting as God is in His own person!

Likewise, the "New Covenant" was not made directly with the church, but in Jeremiah 31:31–34 (along with its repetition in Heb 8 and 10), it was specifically made with the "house of Israel and the house of Judah." God never made a covenant of any sort with the church anywhere in Scripture. Therefore, all the alleged forms of supersessionism must be declared invalid. For example, ecclesiological supersessionism is bankrupt, for the church does not replace Israel, nor do the Christian churches replace the synagogues. If the church was trying to gain credibility in the eyes of the world by claiming the political status that originally was held by the authorities in Israel, they were on the wrong track. In fact, Eusebius' *Oration on Constantine* wrongly identified Roman imperialism with the reign of the Davidic Messiah. Yeshua's kingdom was of an altogether different order from any imperialism this world had or would see coming from the rulers of the nations.

Likewise, theological supersessionism was also incorrect, for grace did not replace law, nor did the New Testament replace the Old Testament. Martin Luther and Rudolf Bultmann both incorrectly argued for a radical opposition between law and grace, but the "grace and truth" that appeared in Jesus Christ (John 1:14) was a direct quote from Exodus 34:6d ("The LORD, the LORD… abounded in grace and truth") at the golden calf fiasco. Furthermore, the first time the Hebrew Scriptures were referred to as the "*Old* Testament," apart from the New Testament, was in the fourth Christian century by Eusebius of Caesarea, where he thereby intended to show the superiority of the new over the older testament. These modern views, unfortunately, go back to the heretical stance of Marcion, who tried to demean the Old Testament by drawing a contrast between the two portions of Scripture that just were not there.

JEWISH–CHRISTIAN POLARIZATION

The whole story about the tragic turn of events between the Jewish and Christian groups is not limited to the enormous and unjustified hate for Israel and the Jewish people that many in the church have raised; this antipathy has affected the work of the church in the process.

When Christianity began to reject its Jewish roots and attempt to replace them with its own story of its origins in the more recent descriptions of its own beginnings, it had the effect of not only forcing a parting of the ways between Jewish followers and followers of the Christian "Way," but Christianity also began to define itself in opposition to the very people that had given them their original heritage—the Jewish people. The church began to lose part of its own story and its shared roots and the grounding it had with Israel. As a result, the church lost its foundation and was now without roots, floating in the air with no history or connection with what God had been doing since the beginning of time and what He would do as He climaxed history—at least according to these new theories. Thus, the effect of such a polarization, said Michael Wyschogrod, was "we have a situation in which both faiths have damaged each other."[47]

---

47 Michael Wyschogrod, "A Jewish View of Christianity," in *Toward a Theological Encounter: Jewish Understanding of Christianity*, ed. Leon Klenicki (New York: Paulist, 1991), 113-14.

Both faiths lost. But the good news of the gospel, announced by Abraham in Genesis 12:3, was that in Abraham's seed, all the nations of the earth should be blessed (cf. Gal 3:8). Both had been set not for damage, but for the grace of God! The good news of the gospel transcended all those vain efforts to do otherwise.

One major attempt to really bring the two sides together came from the pen of Franz Rosenzweig (1886–1929) in a book entitled *The Star of Redemption*,[48] which he began writing in August 1918 on the back of army postal cards as a soldier on the Balkan Front. Rosenzweig spoke with great appreciation for Christianity and the Christian church. While he was at university, he engaged in long and meaningful conversations with Eugen Rosenstock-Huessy, a professor of law and sociology and with his two cousins, Hans and Rudolf. For him, Christianity was a *preparation messianica*, where Yeshua is viewed as a false prophet for the Jews and non-Jews, but whose message nevertheless had positive consequences.

Franz Rosenzweig was agreed that no one could reach God the Father except through Jesus/Yeshua, as John 14:6 stated: "I am the way, the truth and the life; no one comes to the Father but by me." But to this verse he also added another one, where he appealed to Messiah's parable about the prodigal son in Luke 15:31, in which the father said to his eldest son, "Son, you are always with me, and all that is mine is yours." Rosenzweig took from this that Jewish people did not need Jesus/Yeshua to reach the Father; they were already with the Father and thus were in the covenant! Hence, there developed the dual covenant theory: one for the Jewish people and the other for the Gentiles!

Rosenzweig argued that "whether Jesus is the Messiah will be shown when the Messiah comes."[49] In fact, the late David Flusser even allowed that many Jews would not object if the Messiah, when he came again turned out to be the Jew Jesus! However, Yeshua/Jesus who narrates this parable, is as a matter of fact a Jew. That is why it is wholly outside the bounds of proper interpretation to make the elder brother in this parable

---

48 Franz Rosenzweig, *The Star of Redemption* (Boston: Beacon Press, 1972).

49 See this quotation cited in Kai Kjaer-Hansen, "The Problem of the Two-Covenant Theology," *Mishkan* 21 (1994): 52-81, the quote is from p. 71. See also David Flusser, "To What Extent is Jesus a Question for the Jews?" *Concilium* new series, 5/10 (1974).

a Jewish person who already belongs to the Father's house and who has already been included in God's redemptive plan of the covenant, or to incorrectly argue that as elder brother he was without any need for accepting Yeshua as his Savior.

Was it not true that Yeshua's original mission was directed towards His own people Israel through whom the Gentile world would be blessed? Therefore, any dual covenant theory misses the fact that any and all who are included in the covenant must come by faith in Yeshua and His work on the cross, as certified by His resurrection and ascension into heaven.

CONCLUSIONS

What then shall we conclude about Jewish and Christian exclusivity? Arthur Cohen said: "The test of tolerance is where men combat for truth but honor persons."[50] And so it must be here as well. Christians must live up to the theology of love that they espouse, but have, as a matter of fact, failed consistently to demonstrate towards the Jewish people in many notorious places and times in our past history.

Jewish people have had another example of a possible Messiah, rabbi Menachem Mendel Schneerson, who died on June 12, 1994. Many still claim, just as some who had preceded him, that he too was the real Messiah. The Jewish expectation of this small group for the return of Messiah was correct, but such hope must never be placed in a mortal. Schneerson died and has not been heard from since; Yeshua died and rose again from the dead and was seen by his disciples and as many as 500 persons at one time (1 Cor 15)!

Instead, let the claims of Yeshua be subjected to every test possible for his Messiahship. Rabbi Pinchas Lapide was on the right track when he wrote his book on *The Resurrection of Jesus*.[51] He thought the arguments for the resurrection of Yeshua were accurate and historical, but that did not mean that he accepted Jesus' Messiahship for the people of Israel, nor

---

50 Arthur A. Cohen, *The Myth of the Judeo-Christian Tradition* (New York: Schocken Books, 1971), 216.

51 Pinchas Lapide, *The Resurrection of Jesus* (London: SPCK, 1984).

did he accept the Jewish interpretation of the apostle Paul about the resurrection of Jesus as demonstrating his claim to being the Messiah.

So there is where the issue rests to this very present moment. However, Romans 11 still anticipates a coming day in which so massive will the Jewish turning be to accepting Yeshua as the Jewish Messiah that one could say, "All Israel will be saved" (Rom 11:26), for "God's gifts and his call are irrevocable" (Rom 11:29).

CHAPTER 4

WHEN THE RELATIONSHIP BETWEEN THE ISRAEL AND THE NEW CHRISTIAN CHURCH OF THE ABRAHAMIC-DAVIDIC COVENANT WENT SOUR[52]

Replacement theology, as has been often observed, is not a new arrival in the theological arena, for some locate its origins at least as early as the early political-ecclesiastical alliance forged between Eusebius Pamphilius and the Emperor Constantine,[53] who regarded himself as God's representative. In his role as emperor he gathered all the bishops of the early church together on the day of his trl-centennial (thirtieth anniversary of his reign), an event, incidentally, which he saw as the foreshadowing of the eschatological Messianic banquet in the final day. The results of that meeting, in Eusebius' mind, made it unnecessary to distinguish any longer between the church and the empire, for they appeared to merge, as he saw it, into one fulfillment of the kingdom of God on earth in the present

---

52 This article in its first form first appeared some twenty-two years ago in the journal *Mishkan* 21 (1994): 9-20. I am also indebted to Daniel Gruber for his seminal research in his volume *The Church and the Jews: The Biblical Relationshlp* (Springfield, MO: General Council of the Assemblies of God, Intercultural Ministries Department. 1991), 8-10.

53 Eusebius Pamphilius, *The Ecclesiastical History*, trans. Christian Frederick Cruse, Book 3. Chap 36, p. 120 in Gruber, *The Church and the Jews*, 24. Gruber (10) also points to V. Hesich, "Empire-Church Relations and the Third Temptation," *Studia Patrlstica*, Vol IV (Berlin, 1961), 468-69.

time. Such a maneuver, of course, nicely evacuated the role and the significance of the Jewish people in any spiritual kingdom considerations, for that was now the property of the state in this new arrangement with Constantine. Here, according to many, began the long trail of replacement theology as the problem of the state of Israel, with its promises from God were removed from Israel and its promises were made over in just a spiritual form to the church as the new people of God.

Others traced it back even further to the Church Father Justin Martyr, whom we mentioned in the earlier chapters. But surely by the time of Constantine, supersessionism was already in high gear.

Replacement theology, to put a bit more of a definition to it, declared that the church, now seen as mainly the Gentile spiritual seed, had replaced national Israel in that it had transcended and received the terms of blessing in the covenant, which had previously been given to Israel, but which covenant Israel had now lost because of her disobedience.[54] Let us have Tom Wright make the point for us once again as he affirmed:

> Modern attempts to revive such geographical nationalism [as the divine promises in the Abrahamic Covenant], and give [them] a "Christian" coloring, provoke the following, most important theological reflections: the attempt to "carry over" some Old Testament promises about Jerusalem, the land, or the Temple for fulfillment in our day has the same theological shape as the attempt in pre-Reformation Catholicism to think of Christ as being re-crucified in every mass.

He continued:

> The work of Christ is once again "incomplete" [according to this scenario] …. [This] is not only "Christian Zionism," …. it is also, more significantly, Christian Anti-Semitism. If the wrath

---

54 Some, such as my good friend Chris Wright, strenuously objects to the use of the terms "replacement theology" or "supersessionism" as a way to describe the views of this position. In the view of many in this school, the "promise is now being fulfilled through a multi-national people, the Jew and Gentile in Christ, [with] the 'forever' aspects of the nation-state, land, king and priest [being] likewise transcended, taken up, and fulfilled." *A Christian Approach to Old Testament Prophecy Concerning Israel*, ed. P. W. L. Walker (Cambridge: Tyndale, 1992), 6.

of God spoken of by Jesus and Paul was truly *finished* with the awful events of AD 70, then the only appropriate attitude in subsequent generations towards Jews, the Temple, [and] the land of Jerusalem must be one of sorrow or pity .... To that extent "Christian Zionism" is the geographical equivalent of a *soi-disant* "Christian" apartheid, and ought to be rejected as such"[55]

There are at least five fatal flaws, as some are quick to note, in the thinking of those supporting the replacement covenant thesis: 1) The "New Covenant" was made with the "house of Israel and the house of Judah." God never made any type of a formal covenant with the church. 2) Moreover, the failure of the Jews, like the later failure of the church, was calculated in the plan of God (Rom 11:8), therefore Israel's rebellion would not throw God's plan for Israel off track. 3) The New Testament clearly teaches that God has not cast off disobedient Israel (Rom 11:1, 25–26), for they are the natural branches which can be regrafted into the olive tree once they believe, into which olive trunk the Church is also being grafted by faith. 4) The "eternal" aspect of the promise of the land is not to be equated with the "eternal" aspect of the Aaronlc priesthood (1 Chr 23:13), or with the Rechabite descendants (Jer 35:19), as some try to argue to show its temporality rather than its endurance forever; and 5) Paul's allegory of Galatians 4:21–31 does not teach that national Israel has been replaced by the church. Instead, Paul used the method of allegory, not as an exegesis of Genesis texts, but only to teach those who could not get the point Paul was making—that the quest for justification by works leads to bondage, whereas justification by faith and grace leads to freedom and salvation—all of which can be put into an allegory if that is what will make it easier for them to understand. Each of these theses must be examined in as much detail as the space here allows.

THE NEW COVENANT

God never made a covenant with the church as such: the "New Covenant," in which the church now shares, was the very same one that God originally made "with the house of Israel and with the house of Judah" (Jer

---

[55] Tom Wright, "Jerusalem in the New Testament," in *Jerusalem, Past and Present in the Purpose of God*, ed. P. W. L. Walker (Cambridge: Tyndale, 1992), 73-74, 75.

31:31b). No one, to my knowledge, has attempted to make a case for equating "the house of Israel and the house of Judah" as a figurative type or allegorical symbol for the Christian church! In fact, those who argue that such an equation should be made with the church, are unable to establish that any of the seventy-three appearances of the word "Israel" in the New Testament, or the four appearances of "Israelite(s)," are actually equal to the church—not even in one NT text. Moreover, even those who make such a false equation, and who then go about contemporizing the message of the Old Testament, do not make the equation uniformly of all references to "Israel" and "Judah" when they interpret the Old Testament. They do so only when something good is said about "Israel" or where in some traditions there is a tendency to understand that the church is being spoken of in that situation. When something bad, or a curse, is said of "Israel" in the Old Testament, usually that is left as a word remaining for national Israel by modern holders of this theory—a most unsporting way to proceed?

No other covenant made specifically for the church is mentioned in the New Testament. Thus, the New Covenant is a continuation of the plan of God originally given to Abraham and David; it was made with northern and southern Israel, qua "Israel." The gospel presented in the New Covenant was a continuation of God's gracious dealings with Israel: in fact, it was from the Old Testament that the early church got her message of good news/gospel that she proclaimed with such joy in all those years from approximately A.D. 30 to 48, before the New Testament even began to be revealed by God and put in the hands of those who followed the "Way." Thus the church must find its roots in the promises made to Israel or it has no standing and no rootage in history or salvation.

THE FAILURE OF ISRAEL

Israel's disobedience and dispersion were not the end of her calling, for God had announced in the New Testament that his "gifts and his call were irrevocable" (Rom 11:29). In fact, rather than Israel's disobedience serving as a signal that her usefulness in the divine plan had ceased, the apostle Paul asserted the reverse. As Hendrikus Berkhof put it, "She [Israel] is and remains the link between the Messiah and the nations. She could be this link through her obedience, but even now, in her disobedience, she still fulfills her functions as a link."[56] That is why Paul claimed that "because of (Israel's) transgression, salvation has come to the Gentiles" (Rom 11:11).

Another indication that Israel's rejection of the Messiah and her present disobedience (to speak, for the moment, of the vast majority of her people) was not the final episode to the whole drama of her salvation, can be seen in Romans 11:15. Paul argues that, "if Israel's rejection means the reconciliation of the world (in that Gentiles would be given an opportunity to come to the Messiah as never before), what will [Israel's] acceptance mean but life from the dead?" It is possible that this phrase that the passage quoted by Berkhof above ("in her disobedience") could be taken only in a spiritual way, but Scripture does not appear to treat it in that manner.[57] Instead, it appears to be picking up the very figure used by Ezekiel 37:12, 14, where the Lord said, "O my people. I am going to open up your graves and bring you up from them: I will bring you back to the land of Israel ... I will put my Spirit in you and you will live, and I will settle you down in your own land." Thus, the dry bones would be brought back together again and the breath of God would be breathed into the bones of the formerly deceased and dried up nation that had lain scattered all over the valley floor. If some would prefer to treat this passage as a prediction of an individual's bodily resurrection, the divine interpreter himself will disallow it, for that same passage of Ezekiel 37:11 also declared, "Then he said to me: 'Son of man, these bones are *the whole house of Israel*'" (emphasis mine). Therefore, it would be only fair to conclude that Paul was referring to the re-establishment of Israel as God's people in the land again, when he also mentions that Israel's acceptance of her Messiah in the end times will mean what would be like receiving "life from the dead."

But in the meantime, note the logic here. If so much good has come to the world because of Israel's disobedience (in that the Gentiles have, in this interim time period, had the gospel offered to them), exclaims Paul,

---

56   Henrikus Berkhof, *Christ, the Meaning of History*, trans. Lambertus Buurnan (Richmond: Knox 1966), 144-45.

57   "Life from the dead" is never used in a spiritual sense argued Berkhof, *Christ, the Meaning of History*, 144-45.

can anyone imagine what the world will experience when Israel is once again accepted back into the fold of God as believers? Why, it would be like receiving dead people back to life. The reverberations of such an event will indeed be earth-shaking!

But the plan of God had deliberately calculated the failure of Israel and her people. Romans 11:8 affirmed, using the informing theology of Deuteronomy 29:4 and Isaiah 29:10, that "God gave [Israel] a spirit of stupor, eyes so that they could not see, and ears so that they should not hear, to this very day." Thus, the spiritual slumber in which Israel currently tosses in distress is in part divinely induced! God thereby insured, in just that sense, that a portion of Israel would not believe, so that salvation might come to the Gentiles through those Jews who refused to believe. And so it happened that "because of [Israel's] disobedience," divine mercy was shown to the Gentiles—and that condition persists down "to this very day," Paul added.

Of course, there are a large number of Jewish people that do believe; however, the "full number" of Jewish believers (Rom 11:12) will not come "until the full number of the Gentiles has come in" (Rom 11:25). Therefore, it was not a matter of Israel's faithfulness, or her ability to retain what was started with her, that she was chosen by God and made the channel of His blessing to all on earth—nor has it ever been. Such an assessment would need to be made of all the peoples of the world, for as the Psalmist said, "If you, O LORD, kept a record of sins, O LORD, who could stand? But with you there is forgiveness; therefore you are feared." It is God who knows hearts and it is God who gives of his grace so freely.

NATURAL AND WILD OLIVE BRANCHES

Romans 11 Is the *crux interpretum* for all who tackle the problem of the relationship between Israel and the church, and the assumption of some,[58] that "all Israel shall be saved" really refers to the New Testament church, becomes entirely impossible as the chapter proceeds, especially as Romans

---

58 Usually this view is associated with many (but not necessarily all) in the Reformed tradition, for the leading exponents of a premillennial theology at the turn of the century were, interestingly enough, mainly from this tradition of Covenant Theology. For example, see such a Reformation commentator as Martin Luther in his commentary on Romans 11.

11:25–26 goes on. Perhaps this is why many who assume this position, though not all, find it more convenient to ignore Romans 11 altogether in their preaching series on Romans, and instead build their positions on logical extrapolations of their theologies, rather than on explicit exegesis of texts of Scripture at that point.

It is clear from Romans 11:13 that Paul is addressing his remarks in this chapter to Gentiles. It may well have been that Paul sensed that the Gentile Christians unwisely had become a bit arrogant towards the Jewish community, perhaps thinking that God had indeed closed the book on his dealings with this national people with whom he had had such a long history of relations. But that may be the precise reason why Paul began with the rhetorical question in Romans 11:1, "I say then, 'Did God reject his people?'" Paul thunders back his answer: "By no means!" Consider me, he pointedly observes, for I too am from the physical seed of Abraham and the tribe of Benjamin—neither of which is meant to be a means of expressing his identity as having a setting within the Church by such an expression—he meant that he was an authentic Jewish person by birth and heritage.

Paul was not attempting to sustain the general argument of God's faithfulness to all believers, that is to say, that God had not cast off Abraham's spiritual seed, as Paul had allowed in Galatians 3:29, and so he had thereby proved himself faithful. If Paul had meant to say that, what was the point of his raising his physical, tribal ancestry in Israel? No, God still loved the nation Israel, the people whom he "foreknew" (11:2). Consequently, just as God had reserved in Elijah's day a "remnant" of 7000 who had not bowed their knees to Baal, so "at the present time" God also had a "remnant chosen by grace" (11:5) in the nation of Israel. If that remnant in Elijah's day was Jewish, chances were very good that that was the remnant that was meant in Paul's argument. It will make no sense to have Paul arguing that God has Gentile "people" (11:1) of faith out of which he has secured a believing remnant (11:4–5) for himself. The logic would fall under its own weight—who are these Gentile believing "peoples" out of which God has secured an alternate believing remnant?

Paul goes on to distinguish two groups in Israel: 1) "the elect" (11:7) or "chosen" (11:5); and 2) "the rest" or "the others" (11:7). God's grace had given to the first group of Israelites what the second group of Israelites sought, but had not obtained: salvation (11:7).

Now here is the marvel of the whole affair: when the root of a tree is holy, the branches will also be holy (11:l6b). The reference to their roots must be to the promises made to the patriarchs: Abraham, Isaac, and Jacob. Alas, however, "some of the (natural) branches were broken off" (11:17) because of their unbelief. But the temporary loss of these natural branches to the tree resulted in an enormous bonanza for the possible salvation of the Gentiles (11:12). And lest the Gentile believers become too puffed up in their own conceits, as if what they now have in Christ was the result of their own searching and finding, any more than it was of "the rest" of Israel's searching, Paul warns the Gentile believers not to "boast over those branches." For to him the Gentile church does not exist for the sake of the Jews, nor was the root of the church's faith in her, "but the [Jewish] root supports [the Gentile believers]" (11:18). Rather than replacing the former branches, the newly grafted-in branches were anchored and provided for in the promises fixed deep in the roots that had been sunk into the earth—the very promises God had given to the Jewish patriarchs.

In fact, rather than lording it over the unbelieving Jewish branches that had been cut off because of their unbelief, the Gentile believers were reminded that "God is able to graft them [the natural Jewish branches back] in again" (11:23) to the olive tree. It is the Gentile church that is the anomaly here: it represents the wild olive tree that was grafted into the cultivated olive. (Paul realizes that he has reversed the horticultural analogy for the sake of his illustration. Normally wild stock is used as the base on which to graft cultivated branches; that is not the case in his illustration [11:24].) Thus, those who wish to allow Jewish believers to join the new Gentile church as long as they recognize it's superiority misunderstand Paul. Paul sends a warning salvo over the bow such dubious enterprises. Gentiles are not and never were the natural branches: Israel was and still makes up the natural branches!

What then is the answer to the big question? Does God have a plan for physical, national, ethnic Israel in the future? Or is such a hope tantamount, as one writer said, making her a "co-redemptrix"[59] with Christ, or

---

59 So complained John R. Wilch, "The Land and State of Israel in Prophecy and Fulfillment," *Concordia Journal* 8 (1982): 173. See Walter Kaiser, Jr., "Must the Christian Include Israel and Her Land in a Contemporary Theology?" in *Toward Rediscovering the Old Testament* (Grand Rapids: Zondervan, 1987), 46-58.

introducing "Christian Zionism" [60] and "Christian apartheid"[61] into the Bible? Most assuredly not!

Romans 11:25–26 answers that question. "Israel has experienced a hardening in part *until the full number of the Gentiles has come in. And so all Israel will be saved*" (emphasis mine). God is not finished with his people Israel as yet. Therefore to express that he is, not only runs run right in the face of these verses, but also misconstrues the line of continuity that God has built into the whole soteriological process that involved Jew and Gentile from the very beginning (e.g. Rom 1:16), and casts off a balanced doctrine of ecclesiology. Look, therefore, for Israel to suddenly obtain one of these days what she has sought in vain (as far as most of her people are concerned) for all these long years—yet thus far she has not found it. The number of Israelites who will be saved is called the "fullness" (Greek *pleroma*), or as the same word is translated in verse 25. "Full number," exactly paralleling, incidentally, the number of Gentiles = "full number" (v. 25) who have come to the Savior. In fact, Jerusalem will be trodden down until the times of the Gentiles are fulfilled. But then our Lord shall turn once again to his people Israel, as they are restored to their land and given the mercy and grace of God, despite their harsh rebellion all these years against him.

The late Anthony A. Hoekema[62] raised two objections to the way we have argued this passage. First of all, he complained, Romans 11:26 did not say, "And *then* [implying the Greek word *tote* or *epeita*, a temporal usage] all Israel will be saved." Instead, the Greek used (*kai*) *houtos*, meaning "thus," "so", "in this manner," describing the manner in which the events would happen, not the temporal succession of these events. In other words, according to Hoekema, Paul was not saying, "Israel has experienced a hardening in part until the time when the full number of the Gentiles has been reached, and *then* (after this has happened) all Israel will be saved." Instead, Hoekema urged that Paul was saying that Israel has experienced a hardening in part until the full number of the

---

60   See footnote 54.

61   See footnote 54.

62   Anthony A. Hoekema, *The Bible and the Future* (Grand Rapids: Eerdmans, 1979), 144-45.

Gentiles has come in, and in this way all Israel (with Hoekema's new meaning of Israel) will be saved. In other words, the text taught not the timing for this event, but it described the manner in which it would happen—so argued Hoekema.

Hoekema's second objection was that it did an injustice to the word "all" in the clause "all Israel will be saved" to limit this enormous ingathering of Jews to the Messiah, and limit its effectiveness merely to the end times. That generation would be composed of only a fragment of the large number of generations that had been passed by in history in the meantime, so how could one possibly claim that "all Israel" had been redeemed?

Hoekema had been answered, however, thirteen years prior to his writing by another Dutch Reformed theologian Hendrikus Berkhof. To the first objection he replied:

> We do not read "then" or "after this," but there is no reason to exclude the possibility that this "and so" is a future event. Paul is dealing with the historical order of God's activities, and only just before used the conjunction "until" (25). Yet, "and so" implies more than "until." However, it's less clear what the antecedent of "and so" is.[63]

Berkhof went on to suggest that the antecedent of "and so" probably is "until the full number" of the Gentiles has come in (the meaning being that since the "full number" of Gentiles had come in, all Israel could now be saved in that final day). Or, one could read, "and so all Israel will be saved" (meaning, the last would be first, and the first temporarily last).

But the point that both Hoekema and Berkhof missed was that Romans 11:27 linked this "and so" with "this is my covenant with them when I take away their sins." This was nothing less than a reference to the New Covenant (Jer 31:31-34), also called "My Covenant," the "Eternal Covenant," and the "New Heart and New Spirit" in some sixteen other

---

63 Berkhof, *Christ, the Meaning of History*, 145-46.

passages.⁶⁴ The contents of this New Covenant were an expansion of the promises that had been made to Abraham and David and a renewal of the promise that God would send a Seed, i.e., the Messiah, to be their God, and use Israel as his means of blessing all the nations on the earth, and grant them the land as an eternal Inheritance. Thus we are brought back to the land-promise and to the destiny that God has shaped from the beginning for his people Israel (Gen 12:7). Indeed, in the very context from which the New Covenant comes (Jer 31:31–34), there is a renewed emphasis on the land promise once again (Jer 31:35–40)! This promise about the land and the future of the nation Israel could be nullified if the sun and moon were to cease shining; however, in the event that both the sun and the moon continued to shine (I just checked out my window to see if this covenant was still on—and it is!), then for just that same period of time God would continue to maintain his promises which he had named in that context. Even the late highly regarded Reformed theologian John Murray commented, after rightly noticing that Romans 11:26–27 were citations from Isaiah 59:20–21 and Jeremiah 31:34:

> There should be no question but Paul regards these Old Testament passages as applicable to the restoration of Israel. We cannot dissociate this covenantal assurance from the proposition in support of which the text is adduced or from which follows in verse 28 (on account of the patriarchs). Thus the effect is that the future restoration of Israel is certified by nothing less than the certainty belonging to covenantal institutions.⁶⁵

Accordingly, even though the "and so" of this passage in Romans 11 may not be temporal in its reference, nevertheless, it is sequential and/or consequential in that it ties the promises of the patriarchal-Davidic-New Covenant with the coming in of the "full number," or the "full inclusion," of Israel into the one olive tree. Once this is admitted, then the unity and the connectedness of the three elements of Messiah, gospel,

---

64 Walter C. Kaiser, Jr., "The Old Promise and the New Covenant," *Journal of the Evangelical Theological Society* 15 (1972): 1-23. Also reprinted in *The Bible and Its Literary Milieu*, ed. John Maier and Vincent Tollers (Grand Rapids: Eerdmans), 106-20.

65 John Murray, *The Epistle to the Romans*, 2 vols. (Grand Rapids: Eerdmans, 1865), 2: 99-100.

and land come back into play as part of a fully developed theology. Accordingly, the relations between the Jewish believers and the Gentile believers that had gone sour were now healed by the Lord Himself as he would wrap up history.

As for Hoekema's second complaint about limiting the "full Inclusion" solely to the Jewish people of the end times, we can only argue that this is a refusal to see that the past and present remnant of Israel are the foundation and guarantee that God would complete his work in a grand eschatological and climactic act. Repeatedly, the prophets of the Old Testament had depicted an Israelite remnant returning to the land (e.g., Isa 10:20–30) and becoming prominent among the nations (Mic 4:1) in the end day. In fact, Zechariah 10:8–12 is still repeating this same promise in 518 B.C., well after the days when many in Israel had already returned from their Babylonian exile in 538 B.C.

Thus, we conclude that God has not cast off disobedient Israel and replaced her with the Christian church for all time and eternity. The natural branches, meaning present day Israel, must not be regarded as dead and gone forever in the program of God, for one day he will regraft some or all of those natural branches into the trunk from which they were once broken off. In the meantime the wild branches, now the believing Gentiles, must not become proud about their being a new kind of olive tree into which everyone else must be united. God never made a covenant with the church—believe me! The only covenant, and His only plan, was the one He made with the house of Judah and the house of Israel. The roots of the tree of faith still remain anchored in the promises given to the patriarchs. That is the only one available to both Jew and Gentile.

THE QUESTION OF ETERNALITY

The promise of God regarding Israel and her land was said to be an "everlasting" or "eternal" covenant in its scope. But many scholars, such as Chris Wright, admonish us that the expression "forever" (Hebrew, *le olam*) needs to be seen not so much in terms of its "everlastingness" in linear time, "[b]ut rather as an intensive expression within the terms, conditions, and context of the promise concerned."[66] Wright points out that the Rechabltes were promised descendants "forever" (Jer 35:19), but if this were a straightforward prediction, where are their descendants today, queries Wright? In like manner, Wright pointed to the house of David and the Levitical priesthood, in which the same form was used about their longevity in Jeremiah 33:17–22.

However, Jeremiah 35:19 does not use the Hebrew word *le-`olam*, "for-ever" or "everlasting;" instead it uses the expression literally translated, "a man shall not be cut off from before my presence..." The same expression is used of the Levites and David in Jeremiah 33:17. Note, however, when the Hebrew word `*olam* is used of David or the Aaronic line of the Levites, it has reference to the office, not the person, of the Davidic king or the priesthood! And if it be doubted that that is what this Hebrew word signifies, let it be remembered that the promise to the descendants of Israel and the provision of the office of the messianic king and messianic priesthood is as lasting as the sun and moon according to Jeremiah 31:35–40 and 33:17–22.

The careful definition of Daniel Gruber merits close examination. He explained:

> The claim that the Hebrew word for "forever" or "everlasting" really means "to the end of the age" is only partially true. In some cases it does mean that, but that is not all it means. The English word "always" provides a helpful parallel. It means "every time," but it also means "as long as" and "forever."

There are actually several different Hebrew expressions used to signify "forever." Most of them use word `*olam* by itself or with a prefix or suffix. Examples are *me-`olam* (from `*olam*, *le-`olam*, added to `*olam*), and `*olamim* (the plural of `*olam*). Looking at the use of such words in context is most helpful in understanding the meaning that they are given in the Bible.[67]

Gruber then proceeds to show how each of these combinations of the word `*olam* are used in various contexts. First, this word is used to

---

66   Chris Wright, *A Christian Approach to Old Testament Prophecy*, 6.

67   Gruber, *The Church and the Jews*, 339-4l.

express the length of time that God will be God in Genesis 21:33: or that God would be King (Jer 10:10), and His reign would endure (Ps 66:7). Therefore, when God gave the land of Canaan to Israel "for an everlasting possession" (`olam*) in Genesis 17:8 and 48:3, 4, there is a strong presumption in favor of seeing that this promise is just as abiding a promise in linear terms as was true of God Himself, who is "everlasting" and "eternal" (at least so far as what the term could potentially mean). It did not need to be merely an intensive expression within certain boundaries or limits of expression. Here it meant "eternal."

Our point has been to show that the word "forever" is not limited in every instance of its usage, for there are numerous examples of its meaning that transcend such temporal boundaries. When the additional phrases that are used in numerous contexts about the land being given in perpetuity to Israel, and of the enduring nature of God's promises to Israel as a nation are all added up, the impression of all the contexts is overwhelmingly in favor of an oath delivered by God that is as enduring as the continual shining of the sun and moon (e.g., Jer 33:17-22).

THE ALLEGORY OF GALATIANS 4:21-31

Paul's use of allegory in Galatians 4:21–31 has often been understood to teach that the Christian church has now replaced national Israel. But this is to completely misunderstand what Paul intended and the audience to whom he addressed his remarks.[68]

Paul's audience was primarily a Gentile audience. And the issue at hand was whether Gentiles should submit to physical circumcision in order to be righteous before God. If one misses this key point, the meaning of Paul's allegory will be lost and wrong meanings will be found where they previously did not exist.

The comparisons are seen in a series of related pairs: two sons, two cities, two mountains, two conditions, two destinies, and two covenants. Some of these comparisons need to be filled in from one's knowledge of the Scriptures, e.g., Abraham had two sons: one is named Isaac, but the other, Ishmael, is not named in Galatians.

---

68 Here again I am indebted to Daniel Gruber and his remarkable work entitled *The Church and the Jews*. See his discussion on this allegory on pp. 210-12, which I now follow rather closely.

What, then, is Paul trying to say? Is he declaring that the Jews were cast out and that the church is now the heir? To say this would be to confuse the opposites that Paul is using: the opposite of the Jew is not the church, but the Gentile. If one wants to learn what Paul's opposite for the church is, it must be the "unbeliever," not the Jew. For even Paul himself was once a persecutor of those who believed in the Messiah. In that action, he was much like Ishmael, [69] born of the flesh, and destined to be cast out. But when he believed, he became like Isaac, destined to be an heir, and part of the persecuted seed of promise. But the same could be said for a Gentile like Sosthenes, the leader of the synagogue, who at first persecuted Paul in Corinth (Acts 18:17). But when he too became a believer, he moved from one side of this allegory to the other side (1 Cor 1:4).

Gruber aptly concludes:

> The point is not that one's physical ancestry necessarily leads to bondage. For neither Gentiles nor Jews need remain in a lost state. It is the quest for Justification through the works of the law (by both Jew and Gentile, we might add), rather than through grace and faith, that leads to bondage. Paul was writing to Gentiles in Galatia who were making the wrong choice, which would eventually lead them back into bondage and a disinherited state, and eventually turn them into persecutors.[70]

CONCLUSION

Replacement theology, therefore, is just plain bad news for both the church and Israel. It must be stressed repeatedly that the church did not fully evidence a strong belief in such a doctrine until Constantine largely

---

[69] Hans K. La Rondelle, in *The Israel of God in Prophecy: Principles of Prophetic Interpretation* (Berrien Springs, MI, 1983) actually makes the equation that Paul resists: he declared, "This passage has rightly been called 'the sharpest polemic against Jerusalem and Judaism in the New Testament'" (J. C. DeYoung, *Jerusalem in the New Testament* [Kampen: Kok, 1960], 106). Paul goes on so far as to equate "The Present Jerusalem, the nation of Israel, with status before God of Ishmael, who was totally disinherited because he persecuted Isaac."

[70] Gruber, 210-212.

introduced it in the fourth century of the Christian era under a false axis, in which the church and the Empire were forged into an working alliance by the Emperor Constantine and the Church Father Eusebius. The effect was to replace Isaac as the son of promise with Eliezer of Damascus.

But more directly, this substitution and supersessionism of the church for Israel runs directly counter, not only to the repeated expectations of the Old Testament prophets, but also to the painstakingly careful analysis offered by the apostle Paul in Romans 9–11. Instead of viewing Gentiles as being grafted into the stock, root, and trunk of the Jewish olive tree, it reverses the imagery and offers a Gentilized gospel to the Jews. We urge Christ's church to quickly reexamine this most important doctrine, for with it goes not only the investment of the church in Jewish missions and her expectations of God's future work in the eschaton, but more importantly it involves the church's ability to correctly proclaim the doctrine of salvation in its biblical fullness and the doctrine of the church in its relations to Israel and the world. Moreover, it leaves Christ's church helpless before a plethora of Old Testament texts, not to mention before Paul's *magnum opus* of Romans, with its constant reference to Jew and Gentile, in the whole soteriological argument and the definitive emphasis found in Romans 11. The same relations that went sour can be healed by the love that Scripture admonishes Gentile believers to give to all persons, much less to the Jewish people and by the powerful gospel of Yeshua, the Messiah.

CHAPTER 5

WHEN JOHN THE BAPTIST PREPARED THE "WAY" FOR YESHUA

ൕഌ

The entry of Yeshua into the religious life of the first-century Jewish people, and later into the lives of the Gentiles in the Roman world, was strongly linked to the ministry of John the Baptist. Despite John's protest to the contrary, that he saw himself as subordinate to Yeshua, yet for a very brief moment in history, John seemed to appear as the dominant figure.

John the Baptist was the son of an elderly priest named Zachariah and his mother was Elizabeth, a relative of Mary, the mother of Yeshua. Elizabeth, though a sterile woman now past the age of childbearing, surprisingly gave birth to John the Baptist in the twentieth and twenty-second year of the reign of Augustus Caesar (26 B.C.–A.D. 14) (Luke 1:5–24, 39–80; 3:1–2). John's birth signaled a whole new chapter in the ancient covenant and promises of God found in the Old Testament.

Thus, John the Baptist became not only the great forerunner of Yeshua, but according to the Lord Himself, this recluse prophet was the greatest "among those that are born of women" (Matt 11:11). In the Eastern Orthodox Church, John the Baptist is celebrated only second to the Virgin Mary in order of veneration after Yeshua, so great was the church's esteem for him.

However, John, the forerunner of Yeshua, was the epitome of humility and self-renunciation. His testimony to Christ was this: "He must increase, but I must decrease" (John 3:30). And so the life of John the Baptist pictured exactly what he claimed in that statement, for John devoted all of his short life to the One who would come after him, the Messiah Yeshua.

The record of John the Baptist's ministry as a forerunner of Yeshua covers some 194 verses in the four evangelists' Gospels, which in itself is amazing since seventeen of the total twenty-seven books in the New Testament have fewer verses than the total number devoted to John the Baptist in this count of 194 verses![71] However, of this wide-spreading assemblage of verses, a mere thirty verses report any of the words or messages of John the Baptist. But even more amazing is the fact that that number needs to be further modified, for hardly more than half of those thirty verses record distinct or separate utterances, for many of his words are repeated in these thirty verses in the four Synoptic Gospels. Yet the story gets even more interesting and exciting, for in the eighteen to twenty verses that contain distinctive words not repeated elsewhere in the four Gospels, we can identify something over fifty citations or allusions to Old Testament statements, either in formal quotation or just in substance or in essence of what was recorded earlier in the Old Testament. And of these fifty Old Testament references, more than forty of the fifty come from three prophets alone: Isaiah, Malachi and Jeremiah.

Few things are as dramatic and as striking about John as the abruptness with which he appears on the sacred page. In that regard, he appears as suddenly, and without formal introduction as his namesake: Elijah the prophet. Perhaps his sudden introduction was intended to be that way in order that the readers might make the literary connection with Elijah's identical startling and sudden introduction in 1 Kings 17:1.

What makes his abrupt appearance all the more interesting is the fact that he had been preceded by 400 years of revelatory silence from God, during which time the Lord had not sent a prophet or a messenger to his people with his word. However, the Old Testament prophet Isaiah had foretold some 700 years prior to John's appearance on the scene that he would come as a herald of Yeshua the Messiah (Isa 40:3). The same message was repeated 300 years later, when it still was some 400 years

---

71 In Matthew there are forty-seven verses, Mark has twenty-eight, Luke has eighty-five and John thirty-four. The count of 194 is from J. Elder Cumming, *John: the Baptist, Forerunner and Martyr* (London: Marshall Brothers, n.d.), 104-105.

prior to Yeshua's coming, by the Old Testament prophet Malachi (Mal 3:1), that John would announce the coming of Messiah. Furthermore, John's ministry would mark the end of the era of waiting for the appearance of the Messiah, just as he would mark the start or the beginning of the era of the kingdom of God.

John proved to be enormously popular, not just because of what he had to say or because he performed any miracles; in fact John never performed one miracle (John 10:41). Moreover, his ministry did not last more than something like a total of six months. Yet the crowds were attracted to him despite his blunt way of calling for everyone, at all levels of society, to repent and to drop the sin each was so fond of following.

John's goal was to preach repentance, for the arrival of God's reign was imminent. He cried out: "Repent, for the kingdom of heaven is at hand" (Matt 3:2; Mark 1:15). That message seemed to be in fulfillment of how the Essenes at Qumran also had likewise chosen to withdraw from society and take up their residence on the arid shores of the Dead Sea in protest against a society that had forsaken God.

John's career was shortened, however, as Herod Antipas ended it suddenly by having John decapitated. King Herod's displeasure came from John publically announcing that Herod's marriage to his sister-in-law, Herodias, teaching that it was invalid and indeed sinful (Matt 14:3–12; Mark 6:17–29). Josephus, however, offered a different explanation: Herod killed John because he saw John as a potential threat to his regime, since John was becoming so popular and enjoying such a massive number of people who were going out into the desert to hear his message, and John might persuade the people against his own rule or start an uprising against his rule.

THE SOURCES

John the Baptist is mentioned in six early first-century Christian texts. These six would include the four Gospel records of Matthew, Mark, Luke and John, along with the record in the book of Acts of the Apostles. The sixth source would be the work of the Jewish historian named Josephus, who was born about the year of A.D. 37/38, which would put him as living just after the days of Yeshua's earthly journey, since Yeshua was crucified during the prefecture of Pontius Pilate (A.D. 26–36). Josephus died around A.D. 100, after he had served as a general in Galilee during the first Jewish revolt against Rome (A.D. 66–74). But as judged by his own words, he was not much of a general, or a rebel, for he disliked guerrilla tactics, which was the only strategy that worked in fighting against the Romans. Thus, when he and his fellow Jewish generals were besieged by the Romans at Jotapata, Josephus agreed to a suicide pact. However, somehow he survived that pact and instead he surrendered to the Romans. How he ended up with Roman citizenship and a Roman pension cannot be ascertained from the information we possess. However, Josephus apparently was adopted into the imperial Flavian family somehow, for he altered his name to "Flavius Josephus." Josephus himself accounts for all the good fortune that came his way as a result of an incident that involved him shortly after his capture by the Romans. Josephus predicted that Flavian Vespasian and his son Titus would become emperors of Rome, which proved to be correct. This, then, might well account for Josephus' elevation in the Roman society. Moreover, one should also allow for favor to come his way because of his translation efforts that helped the Romans in their conquest of the Jewish people. This did not endear him to his own Jewish people, we can be sure, for rabbinic literature makes no mention of him. His literary works (*The Jewish Antiquities* and *The Jewish Wars*) were probably preserved from destruction because of his brief references to Jesus, James the brother of Jesus, and also to John the Baptist. Because of these references to key Christian leaders, his works may have been preserved by the Christian believers. For example, Josephus' reference to John the Baptist, which is our immediate concern here, came in the *Antiquities of the Jews* 18:116–19:

> 18.116. Now, to some of the Jews the destruction of Herod's army seemed to come from God as a very just recompense, a punishment for what he did to John, who was called the Baptist.
>
> 18.117. For Herod had executed him, though he was a good man and had exhorted the Jews to exercise virtue, both in practicing justice toward one another and in piety toward God, and, so doing, to join in baptism. For thus it seemed to him,

would baptismal washing be acceptable, if it were used not to gain pardon for whatever sins were committed, but as a purification of the body, implying that the soul was already thoroughly cleansed by religious conduct.

18.118. When others also joined the crowds about him—for they were deeply stirred at hearing his words—Herod grew alarmed: such great influence over the people could lead to an uprising, for they seemed ready to do anything John might advise. Accordingly, Herod decided that it would be better to strike first and get rid of him before the insurrection might develop, than to get himself into trouble and be sorry not to have acted once a rebellion had begun.

18.119. And so, due to Herod's suspicions, John was brought in chains to Machaerus, the fortress .... and there put to death. But the Jews believed that the destruction which overtook Herod's army came as a vengeance against Herod [for executing John], God wishing to do him harm.[72]

Prior to Josephus' descriptions recorded in the above citations, he had just finished recounting the defeat of Herod Antipas, ruler and tetrarch of Galilee and of the territory called Perea on the eastern side of the Jordan River. Herod was bested in a battle with the Nabatean King Aretas IV (A.D. 37). However, despite Josephus' mention of John the Baptist, he does not connect him with the ministry of Yeshua.

All four Gospels locate John's ministry in the wilderness, even as Isaiah 40:3 had predicted as the area where he would conduct his ministry. Matthew and Mark note that all Jerusalem and Judea were going out into the wilderness to hear John, including the Pharisees and Sadducees. Luke did not note the presence of these Jewish leaders in John's audience, but he did add that John's audiences included tax collectors and soldiers. But all four Gospels connect John's preaching with the inauguration of Yeshua's ministry. Matthew, Mark and Luke all teach that John's purpose

---

72 Paul L. Maier (trans. and ed.), *Josephus: The Essential Works* (Grand Rapids: Kregel, 1988), 271-72.

in baptizing was for those who acknowledged that they wanted to confess their sin.

The four Gospels all agree that Herod arrested John, but the Gospel of John does not state that Herod executed the Baptist. The reason the Gospels give for the Baptist's execution by decapitation, as already mentioned, was John the Baptist had condemned Herod Antipas for marrying his brother's wife, i.e., his sister-in-law Herodias (Matt 14:3–12; Mark 6:17–29). Josephus, as already noted above, gives John's death a little different spin, for he feared how popular John was becoming with the crowds, thus he could, if he wanted, form to sudden insurrections. Thus, Herod and the Romans were constantly on guard for all such possibilities.

However, it is a wonder that the crowds ever came to hear John, for John did not preach a message that was easy to hear or receive. He labeled his audience with the same pejorative word Isaiah had used of another evil generation in Isaiah 59:5: "You brood of vipers!" John insisted on asking his crowd: "Who advised you to flee from the wrath that is to come?," a question that probably had Isaiah 10:3 in mind. Even with those strong words, John was not finished as yet, for he went on to reprove the tax collectors for their overcharging, their covetousness and their cheating ways. The military men present were rebuked for not getting right with God, and he chastised them for their extortion, their use of violence and their discontent with their wages and the like. Likewise the Pharisees and Sadducees did not escape John's words of condemnation either, for they were both reproved for their love of having pride of place, for their loving to have the seat and place of pre-eminence and their receiving such high respect from the people as well as their pride over teaching the law of God.

All at once the desert no longer was the solitary place, one usually associated with such a desolate place, for the throngs of people were coming from every village, hamlet, and city of Israel to hear this prophet cry out that they all should repent! They should stop taking shelter, John warned, in the fact that they were the sons of Abraham, for they were simultaneously refusing to obey Abraham's God! For too long now, John warned, the Israelites, in a father to son imitation of one another, they had trifled with their privileges and responsibilities. But now the kingdom of God was at hand. It required action on their part and that action began with their repenting before God!

The Baptist also included an eschatological significance to his ministry, for he taught that God would soon come in a future judgment on all, so here was another reason why all must repent and act with justice.

There are seven references to John the Baptist in the sixth source, the book of Acts. The first two references in Acts dealt with the criteria for apostleship. For example, as the remaining eleven disciples searched for a person to fill the vacated spot left by Judas' suicide. Acts 1:21–22 noted that as Peter opened this discussion, he pointed to the fact that they were looking for "one of the men who have been with us the whole time the Lord Jesus was living among us, *beginning from John's baptism* to the time when Jesus was taken from us…" (emphasis mine). Thus these eleven disciples all were eyewitnesses of what they were now proclaiming, but the initiation of John's ministry marked the beginning of Yeshua's ministry. In the second of the seven passages, Peter is again speaking, but this time to a different audience, namely, the Gentiles in Cornelius' household. Once again, Peter presents the work of Yeshua as "beginning in Galilee *after the baptism that John preached*" (Acts 10:37, emphasis mine).

The other five passages in the book of Acts contrast the baptism of John with the baptism of Yeshua. In Acts 1:5, "John baptized with water, but in a few days you will be baptized with the Holy Spirit." In the second of these additional five texts, Peter reports on Gentile Cornelius' baptism in Acts 11:15–16. There Peter recalled the words of Jesus as he began to speak in Cornelius' house about how Jesus said John baptized with water, but he would baptize with the Holy Spirit. That is exactly what Peter saw happen as he preached to this Roman Gentile audience in Cornelius' house, for the Holy Spirit fell on them just as Jesus had said he would.

The remaining three passages all take place in the world outside of Israel. The first occurred at Pisidian Antioch where the apostle Paul ministered in a synagogue on a Sabbath day as Paul asked the audience to compare John with Yeshua (Acts 13:24–25). John the Baptist pointed to Yeshua who came after him as the one people should follow. Then there was a Jew named Apollos from Alexandria who needed to be taught by Priscilla and Aquila, for Apollos knew only the baptism of John as he taught many other things about Yeshua (Acts 18:24–26). Finally, the apostle Paul had to complete the job of teaching Apollos when the two met in Corinth. Clearly Apollos did not know about the teaching on the

Holy Spirit, since he was teaching only about the baptism of John (Acts 19:1–7). Paul completed the needed teaching as his learning was brought up to date.

THE PREACHING OF THE GOSPEL BY JOHN THE BAPTIST

The heart of the message from this stern man out in the desert was simply: "Repent, for the kingdom of heaven has come near." This message had two parts: (1) repentance, which literally meant "a change of mind" in Greek, and (2) the promised messianic kingdom of God was going to appear very soon.

When the crowds asked John what "repentance" meant, he was not at a loss for words. John not only called for godly sorrow over one's past sins, but he also just as boldly called for a reversal of one's direction in life and a complete turning back towards God that gave accompanying evidence of the production of "fruit in keeping with repentance" (Matt 3:8). When some still did not understand what John was getting at (Luke 3:10), he spelled it out in plain terms: tax collectors should not collect more than what they were allowed to take; soldiers were to be satisfied with their pay and stop accusing people falsely. Pharisees and Sadducees should put away their pride and their love of people's recognition; the person owning two coats should share with the person who had none. For at the heart of John's proclamation was his anticipation of the arrival of the Messiah and his kingdom. There had to come a heart change in the people, which would be evident in the way these persons showed it in the type of lives they lived.

John was advocating a new kind of washing, not the same as the washing mentioned in the book of Leviticus in preparation for attending the temple, or as it was used later on for Gentiles' joining the Jewish congregation when they were ready to enter into a covenantal relationship with God. Rather than this being a repeated washing as practiced by many Jewish people, John's baptism signaled that a person was ready to come to God for his deliverance in a once for all washing. God's baptism was about repentance, but it was also about forgiveness. Mark 1:4 and Luke

3:3 called it a "baptism of repentance," therefore they connected it to "forgiveness of sins." It is true, of course, that in the older Jewish doctrine in Isaiah 55:7, sin and repentance were linked, but the new thing was to tie both of these to the rite of washing.

This rite of washing made one ritually clean, for such ritual cleanliness was required if one was to meet God in an acceptable way. Sometimes a Jewish person could be unclean merely from touching an unclean thing, or from a type of bodily emission, so some uncleanness was distinct from sin. But still, this was not an act of hygienic cleanliness; it was a spiritual act!

John's baptism pointed also to a "purging" of the people wherein some would be stored up as wheat was handled in the harvest while others were burned, as happened to the weeds in the wheat harvest. Thus, those who were baptized did so not merely for their own personal confession and reception of salvation, but they did so to join those who espoused to this eschatological hope an expectation of the second coming of Messiah.

Yeshua also accepted His baptism from John's hands. In so doing Yeshua was endorsing John's ministry, his call for repentance, his call for confession of the people's sin, and his call for accountability to God. We would ordinarily think that John ought to be the one endorsing Yeshua, but here the reverse was true. Yeshua endorsed all that John stood for by being baptized by him. The baptism of Yeshua by John the Baptist was attested by the descent of a dove from heaven speaking with a voice that said, "This is my beloved Son in whom I am well pleased," which carried with it explicit allusions to Psalm 2:7 and Isaiah 43:1. Thus, by this action, the Father accredited Yeshua as the Son of God.

CONCLUSIONS

John was Yeshua's forerunner as had been predicted in the prophets Isaiah and Malachi. His six month-long ministry may have been brief, but it was all by way of preparing and clearing the "way" for Yeshua and his three-year ministry that was to follow. John's recognition of Yeshua began as he leaped in the Elizabeth's womb and continued as he preached in the desert, "Repent, for the kingdom of God is at hand."

While some early converts only knew about the baptism of John, yet as they later were taught further, they heard about Yeshua's baptism with the Holy Spirit and ultimately in the final harvest day of the Lord it would be with fire. John was in every sense the forerunner of Yeshua and His message.

CHAPTER 6

WHEN THE JEWISH AND GENTILE CHRISTIANS FLED TO PELLA

Quite a debate rages over the historicity of the reference in the account given of the Jewish believers flight to Pella by the early church historian Eusebius, who wrote about A.D. 325. Eusebius gave us the earliest claim that there was a migration of the Jerusalem "Christians" (to use an anachronistic name for the moment) to the Transjordanian city of Pella, in present day Jordan, just before the destruction of Jerusalem in A.D. 70 (and later again in A.D. 135). This event, if true, would be of enormous interest to those investigating how Jewish and Gentile believers separated and broke apart from each other after being part of a working single entity for so many years immediately following the life and ministry of Yeshua in Israel. [73]

Eusebius' account in his *Ecclesiastical History* (3.5.3) reads:

[T]he people of the Church in Jerusalem were commanded by an oracle given by revelation before the war to those in the city, who were worthy of it, to depart and dwell in one of the cities of Perea, which is called Pella. To it those who believed in Christ migrated from Jerusalem, that when holy men had altogether deserted the royal capital of the Jews and the whole land

---

73 Bastian Van Elderen. "Early Christianity in Transjordan," *Tyndale Bulletin* 45.1 (1994): 97-117. Also see Jonathan Bourgel, "The Jewish Christians' Move from Jerusalem as a Pragmatic Choice," in *Judaism and Early Christianity*, ed. Dan Jaffe (Leiden: Brill, 2010), 107-38. Stephen Bourke, "The Christians' Flight to Pella: True or Tale?" *Biblical Archaeology Review* 39:03 (2013).

of Judea, the judgment of God might at last overtake them for their crimes against Christ and his Apostles and all that generation of the wicked be utterly blotted out from among men.[74]

The identical claim to that which is noted here by Eusebius was reproduced with some slight differences some time later by Epiphanius. For example, the later writer placed Pella in Decapolis, not in Perea, as Eusebius had done. However, Pella was already in the fourth century A.D. within the borders of Decapolis, so that distinction is a rather minor distinction given the vague regional boundary lines marking the borders in that day.

This tradition of a flight to Pella was widely accepted until the mid 1900s when a debate began that has showed little resolution to this day. Archaeological excavations and recent surveys of Pella have been used to reevaluate the evidence for a Jewish Christian presence at this site around A.D. 70, but there was not enough evidence to settle the controversy.

Pella has had a long history, going back to Neolithic times with its earliest mention found in the Egyptian Execration texts of the nineteenth century B.C. under the name of Pihilum. The city of Pella was located on the Wadi Jirm east of the Jordan River about eight miles southeast of Beth-shan. When Alexander the Great conquered the Holy Land around 332 B.C., Greek colonists settled in this area and gave it the Greek name of Pella because it reminded them of the birthplace of Alexander, i.e., the "Pella," which was the capital of Macedonia.

Later in history the city earned a name for itself in church history, as Pella became a refuge for believers, who in A.D. 66 (as we have already noticed above) were fleeing Jerusalem when the Roman armies were on their way to quiet the Jewish revolution. Pella became a Christian stronghold, it was claimed, soon after that.

Pella is in the eastern side of the foothills of the northern part of the Jordan Valley, which overlooks to the west the place where the Jezreel Valley begins at the Jordan River and extends towards the west. The area apparently used for settlement consisted of two hills: a main hill to the north called Khirbat Fahl and one that is higher to the south called Tell

---

74 Eusebius, *The Ecclesiastical History* III.v.3 (Kirsopp Lake, trans., Loeb Series, Books I-V).

el-Husn. Between the two of them runs a valley, Wadi Jirm that drains off to the west down eight miles to the Jordan Valley, which serves a perennial spring that must have originally attracted settlement in this area.

Things began to fall apart for those in Judah and Jerusalem under the two procurators of that territory, Albinus and Gessius Florus. Both of these Roman officials made it their policy to make common cause with the brigands who were overrunning the country of Judah, thus both officials receiving a portion of the spoils in exchange for official protection. As Josephus described the situation in his *Antiquities* (XX.xi.1):

> …there were no bounds set to the nation's miseries; but the unhappy Jews, being unable to bear the devastations which the robbers made among them, were all forced to leave their habitations and flee away, as if they could dwell better anywhere else in the world among foreigners. And why need I say any more, for it was Florus who forced us to take up arms against the Romans, as we thought it better to be destroyed at once than by little and little.

So on account of these unpleasantries, the majority of those who decided to leave Jerusalem were the "Nazarenes," who were led by Simon the son of Cleophas, a first cousin of Jesus, who had succeeded James as the leader of the Jewish Christians. They sought refuge in the neighborhood of Pella. Other Jews, such as moderate members of the Pharisaic party, sought refuge near the seacoast at Jabne under the leadership of Jochanan the son of Zaccai.

Both of these groups, though different from each other, took action to leave Jerusalem because of their belief in the biblical prophecies of the Tanach about the Last Days, which in their view were now being fulfilled before their eyes. They pointed to passages such as Isaiah 10:33–34 and Zechariah 11:1. Why the Jewish Christians took refuge in Pella is not clear. Some have argued that the Nazareth of the New Testament was not in western Galilee, but it was located instead across the Jordan River in the Decapolis. There is no evidence to demonstrate that supposition.

War with Rome was soon declared after this exodus and although the Roman armies experienced a setback at first, Vespasian's forces then conquered Galilee, then northern Judea and finally the walls of Jerusalem were breached. It was because of these events that the words of Jesus in the Olivet Discourse took on special meaning:

> When you see Jerusalem being surrounded by armies, you will know that its desolation is near. Then let those who are in Judea flee to the mountains, let those in the city go out, and let those in the country not enter the city. For this is the time of punishment in fulfillment of all that has been written. How dreadful it will be in those days for pregnant women and nursing mothers! There will be great distress in the land and wrath against this people. They will fall by the sword and will be taken as prisoners to all nations. Jerusalem will be trampled on by the Gentiles until the times of the Gentiles are fulfilled (Luke 21:20-24).

The Roman Empire would feel the mighty hand of God in the future of that final Day of the Lord, but for now the Jewish Christians must hunker down in the mountains of Pella. Yes, the temple was destroyed, the sacrifices ceased, the nation was scattered among the Gentiles and chased away from the gift of the land that God had given to the Jewish people as an inheritance.

THE NAZARENES

But who were these Jewish Christians whom some called "Nazarenes"? The Church Father Irenaeus described them in this way:

> They practice circumcision, persevere in the observance of those customs which are enjoined by the Law, and are so Judaic in their mode of life that they even adore Jerusalem as if it were the house of God. (Irenaeus, *Adv. Haer.* 1.26).

Furthermore, they believed that Jesus was the son of Joseph and Mary, elected to the office of Messiah by virtue of his descent from David and His holy life, which high office was further confirmed at Yeshua's baptism by John the Baptist, when the Holy Spirit as a voice from heaven announced at that baptism: "You are my Son; this day I have begotten you." Moreover, these Jewish Christians announced the kingdom of God and taught that he had laid down his life for the salvation of Israel, after which he was buried and then rose from the dead as he later ascended into heaven from which he would shortly come to set up his kingdom and rule over the house of Jacob.

But according to Epiphanius, the Nazarenes (or Nazoraeans) seceded from the apostolic community in the days of the evangelist Mark. Epiphanius described the Nazarenes as being Jewish people who were attached to the Law and practiced circumcision even though they had come to faith in Christ. They preferred to use Hebrew when reading the Jewish Scriptures and they used a Hebrew version of the Gospel of Matthew. Moreover, they tended to live in Beroea near Coelesyria and in Decapolis near Pella as well as in a place called Cocabe in Bashanitis.

CHAPTER 7

WHEN THE COMMUNITY OF JEWISH CHRISTIANS SLOWLY FELL APART

☙☚

Instead of a sudden extinction of what once was a powerful and respected church of the apostles, the congregations of Jewish believers seemed to be slowly reduced and at times almost forgotten in history. It would be a great find if we knew a bit more about how these closing scenes of separation between the Jewish Christians and the Gentile Christians came about; however, given the successive waves of the Persian and Arab invasions that swept over Israel and Syria, tracing the history of Jewish (as well as Gentile) Christianity during this period, is an impossible feat to say with any form of definiteness.

Every once in a while we hear just tidbits of information where, for example, a Persian commander named Belisarius, had to postpone a battle because the Jews and the Nazarenes (usually seen as a type of Christian group) were unwilling to fight. This seemed to indicate that as late as the seventh century the Nazarenes were still around and numerous enough to be a force to be reckoned with. But already in the fourth Christian century there seemed to be a separation between the Syrian and Transjordanian Jewish Christians. The Syrians, for example, experienced a sort of extinction as the Gentile Syrian Church absorbed them, while the Transjordanian Jewish Christians were almost totally absorbed in the strange sects of the eastern desert. Meanwhile, within Judaism the attractiveness of Hellenization was another factor that was undermining traditional Jewish as well as Christian beliefs.

In the process of all this change, the old names of Ebionite (to refer to some of the Jewish believers) and Nazarene (to refer to other Jewish believers) were giving way to a new phase of life. Jewish Christianity would be carried on further by a succession of individual converts to the Catholic faith.

For example, the story is told of a disputation that took place in Rome in front of both the Emperor Constantine and his wife, the saintly Queen Helena. It featured a debate between the Jews and the Christians. The argument failed to be convincing to either side, so according to the legend, the Jews had to resort to magic. An ox was brought into the disputation and the Jewish leader Sambres whispered the ineffable name of God into its ear, whereby the ox suddenly died and fell at the emperor's feet. For the moment the Jews seemed to be triumphant in the debate, but the famous wonder-working Pope Sylvester was more than a match for this situation, for, as the tradition goes, he asked if the Jews would believe the good news about Yeshua if the ox came back to life again. They of course had no choice but to agree, so Sylvester lifted his eyes to heaven and cried out in a loud voice, "If Yeshua is the true God whom the Christians preached, in the name of Christ, arise ox and stand on your feet." Therewith the ox stood to his feet and began to move about. The Jews gave in and were all baptized. So the legend claimed!

A NEW BRAND OF JEWISH CHRISTIANS[75]

The Jewish people, who were now placing their faith in Yeshua as the Messiah, no longer were coming from the former Nazarene group (which we discussed previously in Chapter VI), but were individuals who were converting to Catholicism. Two persons in the fourth century may be used to epitomize this new group of believers: Epiphanius and Count Joseph.

Epiphanius was born in a Palestinian village by the name of Bezanduca of Jewish parents on both sides of the family in about A.D. 303. Even though his father died when he was quite young, leaving his mother in poor circumstances, a wealthy Jewish friend of the family adopted him and later married him to his only daughter. However, Epiphanius quickly lost his wife and his father-in-law bequeathed to him his extensive

---

[75] Much of the following material was gleaned from Hugh J. Schonfield, *The History of Jewish Christianity* (Oxford: Kemp Hall Press, 1936).

property holdings. While visiting his possessions, he became taken with the charity of a monk he met on this survey of his property. As a result, he became a believer in Yeshua, as his sister. He took an instruction course and was subsequently received into the Catholic Church. He went on to travel in Egypt, where he met some of the Christian Gnostics, who exhibited antinomian tendencies.

He returned to Palestine and founded a monastery in his home town. In the years that followed, he fell into a serious controversy with the school of Origen, especially as represented by John, Bishop of Jerusalem. But around A.D. 368 he became Bishop of Constantia in Cyprus as his reputation for learning increased. In 382 he was summoned to Rome by the emperor to give his opinion on an ecclesiastical dispute. In 394 he was in Jerusalem again as he denounced the use of images painted on a cloth in a Christian church.

He retired to Bethlehem only later to take one more journey to Constantinople in his advanced years to attend a synod gathered to reprimand John Chrysostom for taking in some Egyptian monks, who had been expelled from the church for adhering to Origen's views. Epiphanius, however, did not wait for the synod to convene, but took a ship back to Cyprus where he died while at sea.

Epiphanius' major work was a large volume entitled *Panarion*, an encyclopedia of some eighty Christian and Jewish sects and heresies. It remains one of the key resources on primitive Christian beliefs. Another one of his works was *Biblical Weights and Measures*.

Another Jewish convert that typifies this new kind of convert from Judaism was Count Joseph, as known to us through the record left by Epiphanius. Joseph was a rabbinical student at Tiberias, taught by the Jewish patriarch Hillel II. Joseph witnessed the deathbed confession of Hillel's faith in Yeshua, but it was through the cracks in the closed door, as the Bishop of Tiberias administered to him the sacrament of the Eucharist. After Hillel's death, Joseph found among his things the Hebrew texts of Matthew, John, and the Acts of the Apostles, which Joseph then read and as a result he apparently made his confession of his faith in Yeshua.

When the suspicions increased by the Jewish neighbors that Joseph was a believer in Yeshua, they dragged him into the synagogue and would have beaten him to death had not the bishop intervened. Another later attempt was made on his life by throwing him into the river Cydnus, but he escaped and thereafter made public his confession of Christ. When his story reached Emperor Constantine, he made him a count of the Roman Empire. Later Constantine used Joseph on several commissions, but Joseph spent most of his life building churches in Tiberias, Nazareth, and Sephoris.

But the strong surge of so many anti-Jewish diatribes in writing and the amount of speaking from the Christian community from this fourth century A.D. onwards again had a strong effect on the numbers of genuine conversions to the Christian faith from the Jewish community. There was a steady decrease in the number of Jewish believers in Yeshua. In fact, the very name of Yeshua came to be hated by His very own people. So violent was the disruption of the peace of those times that the Emperor Constantine had to issue a decree of death for those who pursued "baptized" Jews with stones and other forms of physical violence.

Nevertheless, the perception persisted that there was a Jewish peril that labored continuously to refute what they saw as the far-fetched biblical exegesis of the believing church in its rendering of the messianic passages in the Bible. Some non-believing Jews were even willing to attend churches to obtain first-hand evidence of what the Christians were doing, but proving the reality of a sinister secret Jewish world organization that had an anti-Christian mission was difficult to demonstrate, if not impossible to show from the evidence.

The fourth-century church felt their best defense was to isolate the Christian community from the Jewish community. Both East and West church councils met and issued strange policies, as illustrated for example in the "Apostolic Canons." These canons called for excommunication of any clergyman or layman who entered a Jewish synagogue, kept a fast or festival with a Jew, or received any gifts from a Jew.

Even more horrifying were a number of renunciations of one's Judaism required from a Jew if he were to profess faith in Christ. He or she was required to renounce all customs, rites, legalisms, unleavened breads, sacrifices of lambs, prayers, purifications, new moons, Sabbaths, hymns—on and on the list of items went. It is little wonder that the number of Jewish Christians almost came to a total halt, except for those who were "converted" not by the force of Scripture, reason or charity, but now more by intimidation, compulsion, and active violence, rather than the work of the Holy

Spirit. This was not a happy time either for Jewish inquirers or Christian congregants. The rupture between the Jews of the apostolic times and Gentile believers could not have brought more disgrace to the name of Jesus Christ and a greater halt to the number of Jewish believers in the Messiah!

THE HISTORY OF JEWISH CHRISTIANITY FROM THE SEVENTH CENTURY ONWARDS

The intolerance that arose from Gentiles following the fourth Christian century was so severe that Jews would not dare to acknowledge their Jewish extraction for fear they would be persecuted by the Gentiles of whatever stripe. In the meantime, bitter accusations were raised against any remaining Jewish Christians in the believing fellowship.

However, from this time forward, a large number of so-called "converts" were little more than compulsory Christians, whom the Jews quickly labeled as *Anusim* (Jews forced to abandon Judaism against their will), not to be confused with the *Meshumadim* ("apostates"). These compulsory Jewish Christians had gone through a forced Christian baptism in order to escape the confiscation of their goods, as well as the possible loss of their lives. The church was becoming paranoid, for the crime of "Judaizing" often meant one was guilty of nothing more than saying something favorable about the Jews. This could lead to heavy fines or even the loss of one's property and lifelong imprisonment.

Accordingly, the pernicious policy that came in Spain and Portugal, with a brief exception of the times during the Moorish reign, was that the state was forming Christians who were crypto-Christian Jews. As some have said, these Jewish people were bound to Christianity by baptismal waters, but their faith had no more substance than the water. Some have estimated that close to 90,000 Jewish people submitted to this type of forced Christian baptism.

THE CRUSADES

The Jewish people did enjoy a time of peace, however, which began with the conquest of Spain by the Moors and lasted for several centuries. But this time of peace also came to an end for the Jewish people as Peter the Hermit was calling men to join him on the first crusade of what would become a series of seven crusades with numerous additional minor campaigns between A.D. 1095 and 1291. So began one of the strangest anomalies in the history of the Christian church: it seemed as if a madness had seized the cities of the Rhine River, as thousands of Christians set forth to deliver the sepulchral site—and everything else connected with the life of Jesus—from the grasp of those whose hands they judged needed to be avenged for the slain blood of Jesus. This was not a pleasant period of history. It is one of the darkest moments for the reputation of Christianity!

The second crusade was organized by Bernard of Clairvaux in 1147, but it ended in defeat at Damascus. The third crusade was called the Crusade of the Kings, since its leaders were Frederick I, Richard I, and Philip II. Frederick drowned en route and Philip and Richard got to quarreling, so Philip returned to France. The fourth crusade was answered by a few knights who answered Innocent III's call, but this one ended up with the conquest of Constantinople and the setting up of the Latin Empire of Constantinople; the so-called "recovering the Holy Land" was forgotten altogether by this crusade. In the thirteenth century more crusades were attempted such as the Children's Crusade in 1212. But each of these crusades generally failed to achieve their main objective of freeing the Holy Land and its historic sites connected with the gospel from the Muslims and Jewish people.

THE STANDARDIZATION OF REPLACEMENT THEOLOGY

If the fourth Christian century was possibly responsible for the final parting of the ways between Jewish and Gentile believers in Messiah, especially through the writings of St. Augustine and John Chrysostom in that same fourth century, the pronouncements against the Jewish people in the actions of the synods from A.D. 535 to 1434 seemed to once and for all seal that separation as an end to the fellowship of Jewish and Gentile believers in Yeshua. With one council decree after another the church acted as if she were both Israel's jury and judge on all she had come to be and do.

Disappointingly, neither the later Reformation Protestant nor the ongoing Catholic churches acted to reverse the reigning concept of replacement theology, for the greater number of these churches seemed to embrace and preach the insertion of the New Testament church in the seat that was previously held by Israel (also known as "supersessionsim"). Gentile believers were now the new recipients of the blessings originally given to Abraham, Isaac, Jacob and David. In the Reformation era, Martin Luther seemed to many to have surpassed even fourth century A.D. John Chrysostom in his vitriol of anti-Jewish sentiment, so the Reformation Protestant church was given no leadership in changing the bad theology against the Jewish people that had accumulated over the centuries in the Catholic Church. In fact, Adolph Hitler cited Luther with some frequency in his book *Mein Kampf.* The publisher of Hitler's newspaper, *Der Stuermer*, freely quoted Luther in his defense at the Nuremberg Trials after the war. Another, Bishop Martin Sasse of Thuringia, published a work following the Kristallnacht in November 1938, which was a compendium of Luther's anti-Semitic sayings in his writings. This bishop declared Luther as "the greatest anti-Semite of his time, the [one who warned] his people against the Jews." [76]

In spite of the anti-semitism evident during most of the medieval period, and continuing during and after the Reformation, there are indications of Christians from the earliest periods (see chapter 8), who advocated elements of dispensational, and even pro-Jewish ideas in their writings and sermons. This is especially true from the seventeenth and eighteen centuries, long before Darby systematized much of the viewpoint. Watson provides more than 350 quotes from over one-hundred authors:

> My conclusion is that the ideas of philo-Semitism, premillennialism, and even pretribulationism were more prevalent before the nineteenth century than many have supposed. Further, many of those revered by contemporary preterists—such as Westminster Assembly divines, Anglican bishops, and renowned Puritans on both sides of the Atlantic Ocean—were actually premillennialists. While preterists claim that premillennialism is new, it is actually preterism that was considered an innovation in the early eighteenth century.[77]

---

76 Brog, *Standing with Israel*, 35,

77 William C. Watson, *Dispensationalism before Darby: Seventeenth-Century and Eighteenth-Century English Apocalypticism* (Silverton, OR: Lampion Press, 2015), viii.

James Stitzinger, in reviewing the last two thousand years of writings on the rapture, says that beginning in 1648, with the final acceptance of the Protestant Reformation at the Peace of Westphalia, there became a rebirth of premillennialism, says,

> Many Reformers contacted Jewish sources and had learned Hebrew. This moved many of the Reformers to take passages concerning Israel more historically rather than continuing to take them allegorically. This led to more historical or realized eschatological positions among the Reformers. Futurist interpretations including premillennialism began to be more prominent in the church as noted earlier.[78]

THE RISE OF THE PLYMOUTH BRETHREN: JOHN NELSON DARBY[79]

A group of Protestants began meeting in Dublin, Ireland, for prayer and Bible study in 1827–1828. These were church people who had become so disillusioned with their Anglican church leaders and their theology that they felt separation from that Anglican fellowship was necessary. But what made this group distinctive were their views about the Jewish people. They rejected replacement theology (or "supersesssionism") and held instead that God still had a future for the Israel, the same future he had made in his original promises as far back as the days of Abraham in Genesis 12 and 15.

One of their young pastors named John Nelson Darby, who endured a long recuperation from a serious horse riding accident, spent his time studying Scripture. He concluded that when Scripture used the word "Israel," it meant a literal Israel and the promise God had made to them of a Seed, a land and the gospel were also very real. But if Israel was still active in the plan of God, where did that leave the church? Instead of trying to fit both into one plan, Darby concluded God had two separate plans

---

78 James F. Stitzinger, "The Rapture in Twenty Centuries of Biblical Interpretation," TMSJ 13/2 (Fall 2002): 149-171, 160-161.

79 I am beholden to David Brog, *Standing with Israel*, for much of the general outline and a reminder of many of the facts in what follows in this chapter.

for two separate peoples. This became known as the dispensational view of Scripture: God had two peoples and two programs, both of which must be kept separate and distinguished from each other.[80] When Israel rejected their Messiah, God turned to the church and offered them His promises. However, at the time of the second coming of Messiah, God will turn once again in his mercy as he fulfills his promise of giving them the land and fulfilling his promise that "All Israel will be saved" (Rom 11:26).

Darby visited the United States and Canada seven times between 1867 and 1877. In 1875, the first meeting of what would become the annual summer Bible conference movement took place. It was known as the "Niagara Bible Conference." Soon this movement was replicated across America from Atlantic City, New Jersey, to Winona Lake, Indiana, and on to Mt. Hermon, California. This was further strengthened by formation of the Bible school movement, which stretched from coast to coast, such as Philadelphia Bible School (PBS) and the Bible Institute of Los Angeles (BIOLA). Add to these movements the publication in 1909 of the *Scofield Reference Bible*, led by C. I. Scofield, who had studied directly under Darby, and the dispensational view was able to gain an enormous theological foothold in America. The impact of all these initiatives was enormous upon the thinking of a large segment of American theology, but it also added a new sympathetic view for the Jewish people as the number one strategy for the mission of the church (Rom 1:16, "I am not ashamed of the gospel, for it is the power of God unto salvation to everyone who believes: *to the Jew first*, and also to the Greek" [emphasis mine]).

In 1970 Hal Lindsey published a book entitled *The Late Great Planet Earth*, with a dispensational interpretation of prophecy and an argument for the restoration of the nation of Israel back to their own homeland. It directly refuted replacement theology and became one of the best-selling nonfiction books of the 1970s with over twenty million copies sold! That was followed in the 1990s with another series of twelve volumes of fictional stories (along with a children's edition) teaching the rapture of the church at the time of the second coming of Christ entitled *The Left Behind*

---

80   See recent study by William Watson (*Dispensationalism before Darby*, Silverton, OR: Lampion Press, 2015) that demonstrates dispensationalism existed at least two centuries prior to Darby's teaching.

series. Jointly authored by Tim LaHaye and Jerry Jenkins, the series sold over sixty million copies and became the number one all-time best seller.

Today, dispensationalists are not the only group of Christians who reject replacement theology, for a number of major denominations in the aftermath of the Holocaust after World War II, in the days following the middle of the twentieth century, have made similar statements rejecting a supersessionist view. However, now in the second decade of the twenty-first century, support for Israel as a nation seems once again to be dwindling each day as nation after nation and denomination after denomination focus their statements on various ways they are isolating themselves from the nation of Israel. Today, the advent of Christian Zionism seems to be the hallmark mostly of dispensationalists, but there are a host of other Christians—along with some outsiders—who are supporters of Israel as well.

THE ROOTS OF CHRISTIAN ZIONISM[81]

Surprisingly, Christian Zionism predates Jewish Zionism. Some may think that Christian Zionism began with Jerry Falwell and Pat Robertson in the 1980s, but that assessment would be incorrect. The two men most responsible for Christian Zionism were William Hechler and William Blackstone.

But let us switch for a moment to the story as to how the Jewish Zionist movement started. One must first recall the name of Theodor Herzl, a native of Vienna, Austria, who was the Jewish father of the Zionism movement at the close of the nineteenth century. He was at first an advocate for the assimilation of the Jewish population into the European culture, but as he covered the trial in France of Alfred Dreyfus for the newspaper he represented he was shocked by the behavior of the French people and the fact that a debacle was actually taking place in civilized France—the birthplace of the Enlightenment! The only answer left for thinking people, if the Enlightenment and reason would not save the Jewish people, was for the Jews to have their own homeland. Therefore, Herzl wrote a sixty-five page paper in February 1896, entitled in its translation "The Jewish State."

---

81 The term "Christian Zionism" is a name attached to Christian believers in Yeshua who support the creation of a Jewish home in Israel and who antedate and in many cases now even postdate the actual start of Zionism.

The name of Herzl, however, had been preceded by the first of two Christian Zionists named William Hechler, who was born in India to missionary parents in 1845. Though Hechler was not a dispensationalist, in his earlier years he followed the Puritan roots that believed in the restoration of the Jews to their land. When he learned of the Russian czar's edict that forced many thousands of Russian Jews to be homeless by relocation and which led many to their death, he went to Russia to urge Russian Jews to go to the land of Palestine. In 1884 he wrote a pamphlet entitled "The Restoration of the Jews to Palestine according to the Prophets." He thought the time was short, for he incorrectly predicted the Lord's second return would come either in 1897 or 1898!

The other Christian Zionist was William Blackstone, who was born in New York City in 1841. Blackstone received Christ as his Savior at a revival meeting when he was just eleven years old. Blackstone became an enthusiastic supporter of premillennial dispensationalism. It is said he did more to spread the dispensational view than anyone else, perhaps except C. I. Scofield. In 1878, Blackstone wrote the book *Jesus is Coming*, which sold one million copies and was also translated into over forty languages. He, too, rejected replacement theology. Distressed, like Hechler, over the murder and massive relocations of the Russian Jews, he organized Jewish and Christian leaders in Chicago to urge world leaders to intervene in the Russian Jewish problem. Blackstone even crafted what became known as the "Blackstone Memorial," with arguments for the Jewish return to Palestine, to be presented to the United States' President Benjamin Harrison, just as Hechler would also petition the Kaiser of Germany for a similar action.

THREE WHO ASSISTED ISRAEL BECOME A NATION: ARTHUR BALFOUR, WOODROW WILSON, HARRY TRUMAN

When the British leader, Neville Chamberlain, offered Uganda to the Zionists in 1902, his prime minister was Arthur Balfour. The Uganda offer was rejected by the Jewish people, but Arthur Balfour continued to wrestle with the problem of a homeland for the Jewish people as a result of his having met in 1906 with a young chemist from Manchester's Victoria University named Chaim Weizmann.

About ten years later, on November 2, 1917, Balfour, now Britain's new foreign secretary, wrote a letter to Lord Rothschild, head of the British Zionist Federation which read:

> His Majesty's Government views with favour the establishment in Palestine of a national home for the Jewish people, and will use their best endeavors to facilitate the achievement of this object, it being clearly understood that nothing shall be done which may prejudice the civil and religious rights of existing non-Jewish communities in Palestine, or the rights and political status enjoyed by Jews in any other country. [82]

Balfour was a practicing Christian who frequently gathered his family and guests for prayer and Bible study (especially from the Old Testament) in his home. He had a long and distinguished career as a British statesman, but at the end of his life, he regarded what he was able to do for the Jewish people as his proudest achievement.

One of the men who had campaigned for the election of President Woodrow Wilson during his 1912 campaign was Louis Brandeis, a leading American Zionist. President Wilson rewarded Brandeis by nominating him for the U.S. Supreme Court, where Brandeis then served as the first Jewish justice on the bench. When Brandeis learned of William Blackstone's petition to President Harrison in 1891 for the state of Israel, Brandeis urged him to recirculate the "Blackstone Memorial," which Blackstone agreed to do with eighty-two new signatures to the old petition with signatures from Methodist, Baptist, and Presbyterian leaders. This "Blackstone Memorial" was presented to President Wilson on June 30, 1917. Wilson then allowed Brandeis to convey to Lord Balfour and the British cabinet his "entire sympathy" with the concept of creating a homeland for the Jews. This probably had a positive impact on the British passage in November of 1917 of the "Balfour Declaration."

Harry Truman, who began as the Democratic Vice President of the United States serving with President Franklin D. Roosevelt, suddenly

---

82   A paragraph from "The Balfour Declaration," which began as a "declaration of sympathy" with the Jewish Zionist's aspirations!

became President of the United States when FDR suddenly died on April 12, 1945. Truman was badgered by the Jewish Zionists to hear their case, but he liked and granted time only to Chaim Weismann for a presentation of the Jewish cause. Meanwhile, the British were unable to resolve the competing claims over Palestine, so they decided to hand over their mandate to rule Palestine to the United Nations on February 25, 1947. On November 29, 1947, the United Nations voted to partition Palestine between the Arabs and the Jews. At midnight of May 14, 1948, the British Mandate over Palestine formally expired as David Ben Gurion, leader of the Jewish community in what was formerly known as Palestine, read "Israel's Declaration of Independence" in Tel Aviv, Israel. The armies of five Arab nations (Egypt, Iraq, Lebanon, Syria and Jordan) immediately invaded the new state of Israel as Israel's war of independence began. However, just eleven minutes after Israel announced her independence in Tel Aviv, President Harry Truman on behalf of the United States recognized the state of Israel.

THE FUTURE OF JEWISH–CHRISTIAN RELATIONS?

A host of names in the evangelical world rises to the surface as those who espouse the cause of the state of Israel to survive and prosper in the face of numerous Arab threats. But while this support is generally appreciated by Israelis, many non-Christians worry what the motive for this support is. The Jewish people fear assimilation by Christian conversion and marriage. There is little, if any, memory of the Jewish roots of Messiah or the Jewish writings of both testaments. The message of Isaiah 52:13–53:12, for example, has been avoided for too long in the Jewish community, for this is one prophetic reading that is studiously avoided in their public readings from the prophets in the synagogue. But here is a possible center for a recovery of all that once flourished in the first four centuries of the common era.

CHAPTER 8

WHEN THE EFFECTS OF REPLACEMENT THEOLOGY ARE REALIZED IN OUR SYSTEMATIC THEOLOGY

☙

Some may wonder, "Really, what difference does it make if our theologies contain a vacuum, or an absence, in them with regard to the future of Israel?" Of course, this question does not mean to imply, or to state forthrightly, that racial prejudice can be indulged in by a Christian. No, that would be a sin against God and mankind. But isn't it possible to highlight the work of Christ in his church, some will plead, without our being required to fit the Jewish question into that theology? Most systematic theologies do not treat Israel, or God's covenants with them, so why should we be concerned to do so?

My thinking on such questions, as those just posed, was enhanced and enlarged by reading Ronald E. Diprose's work *Israel and the Church: The Origin and Effects of Replacement Theology*. He began his book by disapproving of those who had made the issue of Israel somewhat of a theological football that theologians could kick around as suited their own interests. For example, as we all know, dispensational theologians made ethnic Israel very important for their theologies, while Reformed theologians tended to feel that it was more important to show that promises made to Israel were now completely eclipsed by God's new concern with church. Furthermore, to make institutional distinctions between the church and Israel, as dispensationalists do, was equivalent to identifying oneself with a dispensational theology.

It is important to note than even before dispensationalism became popular in Britain around A.D. 1830,[83] the two different views concerning Israel's relevancy to the church today had almost as long a history as the history of the church itself.[84] Thus, the issue of the enduring relevancy of the divine promises made to Israel have often been vigorously debated in the history of the Church ever since the second century A.D. Why then after all this time should a Christian be concerned with this question? Are there not bigger and more important issues to cover than this one, which seems so peripheral?

But there is another reason why the question of Israel and the church has come back in the twenty-first century demanding answers from both Israel and the church. Two brand new events in our recent history have given us a whole new urgency to this question: (1) the *Shoah*[85] in Nazi Germany, and (2) the announcement of the recognition of the new, modern state of Israel on May 14, 1948. Therefore, the two opposing views briefly noted above both faced special challenges which had enormous implications for the resulting view of hermeneutics of Scripture, along with serious repercussions in missiology, soteriology, ecclesiology and eschatology. So the question of Israel was not just a single issue that only touched the Jewish question; no, it could mean that many systematic theologies have been skewed and have missed a key element in their various books. However, the

---

83 See Watson, *Dispensationalism before Darby*.

84 Recent studies by Medieval scholar Francis X. Gumerlock, Timothy J. Demy, and Thomas D. Ice, and William Watson, to mention a few, demonstrate that dispensational ideas were believed at least from the third century through the Reformation, before their systematization by Darby. See the non-dispensationalist scholar Francis X. Gumerlock on a third century work called *The Apoclypse of Elijah* ("The Rapture in the *Apocalypse of Elijah*," *Bibliotheca Sacra*, 170 (October-December 2013), 418-431); Demy and Ice write on a seventh century sermon by Pseudo-Ephraem (Timothy J. Demy and Thomas D. Ice, "The Rapture and an Early Medieval Citation," *Bibliotheca Sacra*, 152 (July-September 1995): 306-17); See also Paul J. Alexander, *The Byzantine Apocalyptic Tradition*, trans. and ed. by Dorothy deF. Abrahamse (Berkeley, CA: University of California Press, 1985), 210; in reference to a rapture citation in the fourteenth century, see Gumerlock's article, *The History of Brother Dolcino* ("A Rapture Citation in the Fourteenth Century," *Bibliotheca Sacra* 159 (July-September 2002: 349-362).

85 The Hebrew term for the Holocaust meaning "desolation" is used to describe one of the most noxious atrocities ever carried out against the Jewish people. This was Adolph Hitler's plan in his "Final Solution:" "to ensure that no longer would there be a single Jew upon Planet Earth."

Shoah and the birth of the modern state of Israel have given the church and its leaders an opportunity to rethink the issues as never before in the history of the church. Therefore, It will not be possible for works of systematic theology to continue to omit Israel as many have in the past (or to make only a marginal reference to Israel's theological significance) in their setting forth the doctrines of the Christian faith. As Gordon Lewis and Bruce A. Demarest stated in their systematic theology: "The notion of institutional Israel is a missing link in much of Christian theology."[86] In fact, Israel's absence from all too much of Christian theology is a fact that cries out to God for his mercy and his forgiveness, as well as the same from the people who have faced suffering and hardship most of their existence. But the apostle Paul did not shrink back from discussing this issue, for he found it to be a key part of the divine plan of salvation in Romans 9–11. Our plea, then, as it was for Diprose in his book, that the Christian church should now take up the question of Israel, not as being a part of any one theological system, but for its own sake. Failure to do so has brought great damage to Christian doctrine and practice, as we will attempt to outline here.

One of the ways in which Christian theology has been damaged is in the way all too many Roman Catholic and Reformed interpreters have rendered the meaning of Israel in the Old Testament by using the allegorical method of interpretation. This tended to set the Bible in a Greek philosophical pattern, which resulted in a loss of a Jewish worldview and the divine point of view. Another area, where such a pushing aside the Jewish nation showed a glaring weakness in our theologizing, was when the medieval church had members who advocated the destruction of images and icons by the church, but who were often quickly silenced by others who charged that those who opposed the use of images and icons in the church were people "who thought like a Jew," or who were persons with "a Jewish mind." As a result the medieval church paid no attention to the second command in the Decalogue against making images of God or of any other thing in creation. This, however, was only the beginning of our troubles in the Church!

---

86 Gordon R. Lewis and Bruce A. Demarest, *Integrative Theology*, 3 vols. (Grand Rapids, MI: Eerdmans, 1994), 3:336.

THE STORY OF GOD'S UNCONDITIONAL COVENANT

The theology of the Bible does not come with an academic set of propositions or affirmations that are already itemized for us in outlines or propositions, but the Bible's theology is set in the grand story of how God called a man named Abram, living in Ur of the Chaldees, one whom He promised to bless, even as He designated him to be the transmitter and agent of the divine promise-plan through whom God would bless the rest of humanity. The Lord made Abram into a nation and rescued that nation from the hands of the most powerful nation that world had up to that time: Egypt. God initiated this plan by calling this Semite from Ur of the Chaldees to trust him and to move to a land He would show him to be his new home. What must be carefully noticed, however, is the promissory and unconditional nature of God's covenant with Abram, which set of blessings and promises He continued to extend to Isaac and Jacob.

After more than two centuries of nurturing the three patriarchs on the plan of God, the Lord multiplied Israel so bountifully that they became a large nation. But they became enslaved by Egyptian bondage that drew them into hard labor. But God revealed his presence and power on behalf of his elect people and they left Egypt en masse and wandered in the desert for forty years before being given the signal that it was now the right time to go up against the Canaanites in conquest of the Promised Land, which they did even though they left much of the work of conquering the land and its people unfinished.

Later, God gave prophets like Samuel, Elijah and Elisha to Israel, along with his choice of a king He favored, a shepherd boy from Bethlehem named David, the son of Jesse. But the nation divided after David's son Solomon ruled for forty years. Israel fell into deep immorality and idolatry. Yet God refused to give up on this nation. Israel's uniqueness was to be seen in her relationship to God and her unprecedented covenant between the Lord and His people Israel.

Israel survived, not because of her own faithfulness to God, but because the Lord was faithful to His promise to Abraham—God was not a man that he should lie! The kingdom of Judah likewise survived in spite of her awful record of constant disobedience (2 Sam 7:16; 23:5; Ps 89:3–4; 132:10–18). Israel and Judah were exiled, not in Egypt as before, but this time in Assyria and Babylon. Nevertheless, God would restore her back to her land once more in "that day" (Jer 30:3; 31:10–11, 35–37). Israel would be just as permanently part of the promise-plan of God as the new heavens and new earth were permanently in the cosmos (Isa 66:22). The people might (and did) change, but God remained true to His word, for He was God!

Scripture surprises us in a way, for given Israel's poor track record on obeying the Lord, we would think Israel had gone too far away from God, yet Jesus, when He came in his first coming, restricted His ministry almost exclusively to Israel. Why? It was because He was going to keep His word of promise to the Jewish people. But never was there any desire expressed by our Lord that He would abandon Israel because of their blatant sin and rebellion against Him. In fact, Paul grapples with questions such as these: Is the good news of God's grace merely the result of the imagination of the Jewish people, or was He still calling Israel to faith and repentance? Or must God stick to His ancient promise regardless of how poorly Israel failed to respond? Why had God made this one people the center of His sovereign promise-plan from Genesis to Revelation?

But if we look at how things turned out with Israel's faithlessness, why couldn't God simply abandon His people Israel and just start over with something like the church? Don't Christians sort of imply that this is what has happened anyway? No, God could not lie and turn back on His own word promised to Abraham, Isaac, Jacob and David. Moreover, Israel temporarily became the "enemies of the gospel" so that the Gentiles (Rom 11:13, 28a) also might receive the good news as it had come to Israel.

Paul argued on these questions in this manner: But as far as the "election [of God] is concerned, they are loved on account of the patriarchs, for God's gifts and his call are irrevocable" (11:28b-29). There just was no way the ancient plan was going to collapse or go out of style! The full working out of the promise-plan of God never has (nor will it) depend on Israel's faithfulness to the Lord and His word, but it will rest forever solely on God's faithfulness to His own promise and His grace and mercy.

The marvel is that Israel continued to exist all those years, from the 586 B.C. destruction of the temple and the city of Jerusalem up into the twenty-first century. This is a marvel of God's sustaining power. Just consider, how many Girgashites do we know today? How many Canaanites?

How many Amorites? How many Jebusites? They all perished and the memory of them is preserved only in the pages of Israel's history. But the name and people of Israel has survived contrary to all other nations that once were on planet earth. Why?

REPLACEMENT THEOLOGY AND THE NEW TESTAMENT

According to the unbiblical concept of replacement theology, Israel has been repudiated and disowned by God and has now been replaced by the divine favor on the church in the plan of God. There is no question but that the church stands in a revelational continuity with Israel in the plan of God, but that fact does not imply or teach that the original status and promises given to her from the very beginning of her days in the plan of God have now been taken away from her because she has stumbled and rebelled against God. When God's plan added the church, this did not mean that He therefore needed to jettison His people Israel in order to make room for the church! In fact, Israel would be the channel for any and all the church would receive.

It is important, then, to link Jewish particularism (as some regard it) with God's universal plan to include the believing Gentiles with believing Jewish people, as it was first affirmed in Genesis 12:2–3. It would be through Jewish particularism that God would extend His salvation and demonstrate His universal purpose for all mankind. The small amount of conflict between the church and the synagogue that appears in the New Testament was more of an in-house debate among brothers rather than a major breach in the plan of God. It would be wrong to argue from these occasional disputes in the New Testament with some of the Jews to some form of replacement theology in our interpretation of Scripture.

For instance, Jesus in His discussion with the Samaritan woman in John 4 argued that the Jews (among whom Jesus definitely counted himself [4:9]), possessed a unique knowledge of God (4:22). Only as a Jew Himself could Jesus contribute to God's saving work (4:42). Thus, the whole world is indebted to the Jewish nation for the salvation that has come in Christ the Messiah via the Jewish people.

The question of Israel's position with regard to the believing Church is given its most public airing in Romans 9–11. Paul's opening statement in 9:1–5 makes it clear that his use of the term "Israel" refers to an ethnic group of people, and therefore was not as a cryptic way of referring to the Christian church under Israel as a symbol for the church.

Thus, "it is not as though God's word had failed" (9:6a) just because Gentiles were now entering into the believing body. Paul will use the name "Israel" eleven times in this text. Of course, allowed Paul, "not all who descended from Israel are Israel" (9:6b). Accordingly, we observe two usages of the word "Israel": in the first six verses an "Israelite" is part of the remnant, which were chosen in the grace of God; in the remaining verses "Israel" is used of the unbelieving majority in that nation.

Paul opened up this whole discussion with a rhetorical question that required a negative response: "I ask then, Did God reject his people?" (11:1). That is very same question posed by replacement theology. Paul's answer is clear: "Absolutely not!" (11:1). Furthermore, Paul himself was also a descendant of Abraham, and one who came from the tribe of Benjamin. So let it be clearly stated: "God did not reject His people" (11:2). All who argue the reverse position take a stance that is boldly in the face of Scripture's claims. No one can argue that Israel is now out of the picture; it is not!

But if it were argued that Israel has as a matter of fact "stumbled" and "fallen beyond recovery" (11:11), Paul strongly opposes that view as well (11:11b). Just as Gentiles have received mercy from God, so Israel too will receive mercy from God (11:30). That is God's prerogative, not ours!

Others wish to re-interpret what was taught in the Old Testament by their reading of the New Testament eisegetically. But here once again this is an improper move to form a new canon within a canon. This move must be resisted despite some good motives that may be driving such a hermeneutical shift. The Old Testament text must be revered and honored as the abiding word of God and in vogue as stated until God Himself signals otherwise—such as some parts of the Old Testament cult and liturgy (Exod 25–Lev 27) were to be phased out by his work on the cross. But these places are clearly marked in Scripture from the get-go. Such was true in the case of the tabernacle and its services. In this case we are told already in Exodus 25:8, 40 that the tabernacle was to be built according to "the pattern/model shown Moses." There was the hint that God had a built-in obsolescence in Israel's worship. The "real" remained in heaven or with God and the "model" or the "pattern" was in-play only as the Lord determined, or until the Lord Himself presented the actual or the "real" counterpart to Israel and to our day.

REPLACEMENT THEOLOGY AND ECCLESIOLOGY

I am once again indebted to Diprose[87] (his chapter 4) for his fine discussion of the implications of adopting a view favoring replacement theology for our current view of the church. Diprose began by noting that Origen regarded the body of Israel as mere types of spiritual Israelites, which he was quick to say was the "church." This disinheritance of Israel by the church set off a series of repercussions for the structure of the church and its ministries.

Yeshua had promised that he would build His "church" so that it would withstand any and all opposition (Matt 16:18). To carry this promise out, the Holy Spirit revealed to the new group of believers after Yeshua's ascension into heaven that the role of "elders," who had been a part of Israel's life, would now also be a part of the apostolic church (Acts 11:30; 15:2, 22-23). Accordingly Paul and Barnabas introduced the same into the new centers of worship now being formed. The job of these elders, also called "presbyters," was to oversee God's people. This task of "overseer" was also known as "bishop" (Acts 20:17, 28; Phil 1:1; 2 Tim 3:1). There was another group known as "deacons" whose duties were more restricted than those of the elders. Thus, a two-tier concept of the ministry developed. But what is important to note here is that some thought the New Testament had invested those called elders with a *priestly* function, which set them apart from the rest of the church. However, this group was not called upon to mediate between God and other church members as the priesthood had in olden times. In fact, Peter and the writer of Hebrews made it clear that the priesthood was now the prerogative of all members of God's spiritual house, over which He as Messiah, Lord and King presides (1 Pet 2:1-10; Heb 3:1-6; 4:14-16; 7:11-10:23). Jesus Christ Himself was the *only one* who now had a priestly function!

---

87 Diprose, Ronald E., *Israel and the Church: The Origin and Effects of Replacement Theology* (Waynesboro, GA: Authentic Media, 2000).

For those who saw the church as a replacement for Israel there was a tendency to apply many of the Old Testament concepts to the church. Thus, ministers or pastors in those churches were regarded as the true *priestly* race of God. The bishop was presumed to have special powers granted to him from God. Thus he was the only one who could perform baptisms. Moreover, in the celebration of the Eucharist, the table was referred to as an "altar" and the elements on the table as a "sacrifice." This, however, tends to downgrade Christ's sacrifice, as it is argued that the bread and wine are actually transformed into the body and blood of Christ. All too often the church indiscriminately took over the liturgical practices of the Old Testament and gave them a spin from Old Testament times to their new location in the New Testament. It can be seen at this distance in space and time, that once replacement theology is adopted, very little if anything can prevent the church from appropriating Old Testament cultic practices into the life of church.

To illustrate this point, notice how the emperor Constantine, who became a Christian early in the fourth Christian century, began a tradition of convening church councils. For example, he convened the Council of Nicea in A.D. 325, whose main purpose was to overthrow Arianism, which reduced the eternality and deity of Christ. This overthrow helped the church immensely. But there were other questions taken up at same time. In a letter Constantine sent to all those church leaders who could not able to attend Nicea, he wrote,

> It was declared to be particularly unworthy for [Easter], the holiest of all festivals, to follow the [calculation] of the Jews, who had soiled their hands with the most fearful of crimes, and whose minds were blinded ... We ought not therefore, to have anything in common with the Jews ... we desire, dearest brethren, to separate ourselves from the detestable company of the Jews... [even if their deliberations were not wrong] it would still be your duty not to tarnish your soul by communications with such wicked people. [88]

---

88 "On the Keeping of Easter," *NPNF* 14.54 (Schaff).

Such an action seems to be contrary to the liturgical direction many in the church were going in the fourth Christian century. But since the Old Testament liturgy, the temple, and the sacrificial cult had come to an abrupt end—both in Christ's death and resurrection and with the military success of Rome—therefore it was safe to indulge in what were now passé forms of worship. But with the Passover still being observed in the Jewish community, the risk of this institution being a bridge over which believers could be attracted back into Judaism was too great! Therefore, the church opposed it.

REPLACEMENT THEOLOGY AND ESCHATOLOGY

As the church tried to perceive her role in history, the fourth-century eclipse of millenarianism in the first three Christian centuries produced an earth-bound medieval theocracy, as Diprose correctly argued. It happened, therefore, that the promised future kingdom of God was completely assimilated into the present-day life of the church. But this process of assimilation by the church was not found anywhere in the New Testament. Some wanted to argue that the promises of the Old Testament had been completely fulfilled in Christ's saving work in the church. To show this was so, Christ and the church were depicted as antitypes of Old Testament institutions. This is why Israel was the only nation to develop an eschatology in the ancient Near East. According to this mixed-up view, Jesus is "Israel" and his resurrection is Israel's "restoration" back in the land. This view assumes that the end of all things will be limited to judgment seat of Christ; there would be no restoration of the nation Israel to their homeland, no salvation of "all Israel," and no rule and reign of Yeshua on earth!

However, Paul unveiled a "mystery" about Israel's future so that the Gentile readers would "not be conceited" (11:25). It was simply this: Israel has experienced a hardening in part until the full number of the Gentiles had come to Christ (11:25–27). But Israel would seek to return to the Lord in the last days. At that end time "All Israel will be saved" (11:26).

So while the church felt the need to celebrate her own date for Easter and not locate Easter on the dates of the Jewish Passover, yet she built much of the church's organization and practices on the levitical themes described in the Torah. Some of these themes included a sacramental view of baptism and a sacramental view of the Eucharist.

CONCLUSIONS AND LESSONS LEARNED

By now it is clear that many systematic theologies give scant attention to Israel in their theologies. This neglect was often connected with what came to be known as replacement theology. It became popular to give to the church what had previously been given to Israel.

Despite these new paths laid out by the church, the apostle Paul strongly affirmed Israel's status and calling in Romans 9–11. Even though the view that the church had completely replaced Israel in the promise-plan of God, Paul, both by his practice and by his teaching, affirmed the reverse of replacement theology. Such a disinheriting of Israel unfortunately did not remain the only element that needed correction in Christian thought; it also affected the Bible's view of the church and her view of the future.

Replacement theologians made the older testament into a thoroughly Christian book as they re-interpreted texts such as Malachi 1:10-12 to confirm their own point of view. Moreover, the tendency was to call some leaders in the church "priests" in order to stress a new concept of the ministry as being one that was "sacrificial" in its impact rather than stressing it as a call to the proclamation of the word. But the New Covenant had stressed instead the sufficiency of Christ's once-for-all sacrifice; it had emphasized the priesthood of all believers as it had also focused on faith in Messiah as the only means of personal salvation!

Replacement theology had other negative influences, for it denied Israel was an elect people of God. The church was taught that she was the normative expression of the promise of the messianic kingdom. But if the church was now living in the anticipated kingdom of God, where was the promised peace and righteousness on earth? Instead, the church in the Middle Ages proved itself to arrogant and self-serving. From Constantine's time forward, often the disinheriting of Israel was backed-up by violence and various forms of ecclesiastical legislation that played directly into the actions that supported violence against the Jewish people (anti-Semitism).

Also affected was the divine promise that Israel would be restored to her land once again, which was often rejected by many in the nation, would be joined together as one people; Messiah would return to earth to set up His rule and reign on earth for a thousand years; and that faith in Yeshua, the Messiah, was the only way to life everlasting.

The worse effect replacement theology had on Christian theology and thinking was the corollary that much of the Old Testament had to be rendered or interpreted allegorically. Along with this change, there also was a selective use of Old Testament texts.

Our concern, expressed by Diprose as well, is this:

> *Christian theology must be based on sound hermeneutical principles which presuppose the Church's essential relationship with Israel.* These include taking into account the whole of the biblical Canon, taking seriously the Jewishness of Jesus and of much of the New Testament.[89]

Our hope is that our post-Holocaust theologies will reflect what Scripture promised Israel as part of their systematic overviews of biblical theology. We must rid our theologies of those elements in them that presuppose a replacement theology and lead to a supersessionism.

---

89 Diprose, 172.

BIBLIOGRAPHY

Berger, David, "Jewish-Christian Relations: A Jewish Perspective," *Journal of Ecumenical Studies* 20:1 (1983).

Brog, David. *Standing With Israel: Why Christians Support the Jewish State.* Lake Mary, FL: Front Line, 2006.

Bolender, Merrill. *When the Cross Became a Sword: The Origin and Consequences of Replacement Theology.* 2nd ed.. Indianapolis, IN: Psalm 71:18 Publishing, 2011.

Brown, Michael I. *Our Hands are Stained with Blood: The Tragic Story of the Church and the Jewish People.* Shippensburg, PA: Destiny Image Publishers, 1992.

Bulgakov, Sergius. *The Friend of the Bridegroom: On the Orthodox Veneration of the Forerunner.* Trans. Boris Jakim. Grand Rapids: Eerdmans, 2003.

Burge, Gary M. *Whose Land? Whose Promise? What Christians Are Not Being Told about Israel and the Palestinians.* Cleveland, OH: Pilgrim, 2003.

Callin, Terrance. *Forgetting the Root: The Emergence of Christianity from Judaism.* Mahwah, NJ: Paulist, 1986.

Cohen, Chuck and Karen. *Our Return to Biblical Roots.* Lancaster, LA: Sovereign World Ltd., 2007.

Crossan, John Dominic, and Jonathan L. Reed. *Excavating Jesus: Beneath the Stones, Behind the Texts.* San Francisco: Harper San Francisco, 2001.

Diprose, Ronald E. *Israel and the Church: The Origin and Effects of Replacement Theology*. Waynesboro, GA: Authentic Media, 2000.

Doukham, Jacques B. *Israel and the Church: Two Voices for the Same God*. Peabody, MA: Hendrickson, 2002.

Dumbrell, W. J. *Covenant and Creation: A Theology of Old Testament Covenants*. Nashville, TN: Thomas Nelson, 1984.

Dunn, James D. G. *A New Perspective on Jesus: What the Quest for the Historical Jesus Missed*. Grand Rapids: Baker, 2005.

Ellisen, Stanley A. *Who Owns the Land?* Portland, OR: Multnomah, 1991.

Flusser, David. "To What Extent is Jesus a Question for the Jews? *Concilcium* new series, 5:10 (1974).

Goldberg, Louis. *Are There Two Ways of Atonement?* Baltimore: Lederer, 1990.

Goldhagen, Daniel Jonah. *Hitler's Willing Executioners*. New York: Random House, 1997.

Gruber, Dan. *The Church and the Jews: The Biblical Relationship*. Hagerstown, MD: Serenity, 1997.

Hagner, Donald A. *The Jewish Reclamation of Jesus: An Analysis of the Modern Jewish Study of Jesus*. Grand Rapids: Zondervan, 1984.

Holwerda, David E. *Jesus & Israel: One Covenant or Two?* Grand Rapids: Eerdmans, 1995.

Horner, Barry E. *Future Israel: Why Christian Anti-Judaism Must Be Challenged?* Nashville, TN: B & H, 2007.

House, H. Wayne, ed. *Israel: The Land and the People: And Evangelical Affirmation of God's Promises*. Grand Rapids: Kregel, 1998.

Juster, Daniel C. *Passion for Israel: A Short History of the Evangelical Church's Commitment to the Jewish People and Israel*. Clarksville, MD: Messianic Jewish, 2012.

Kai, Kjoer-Hansen. "The Problem of Two-Covenant Theology," *Mishkan* 21.2 (1994): 52-81.

Kaiser, Walter C., Jr. "The Assessment of 'Replacement Theology,'" *Mishkan* 21(1994): 9-20.

_____. "The Land of Israel and the Future Return (Zechariah 10:6-12)," in *Israel: The Land and the People*, 209-30. Ed. H. Wayne House, Grand Rapids: Kregel, 1998.

_____. "Jewish Evangelism in the New Millennium in Light of Israel's Future (Romans 9–11)," in *To the Jew First: The Case for Jewish Evangelism in Scripture and History*, 40-52. Ed. Darrell L. Bock and Mitch Glaser, eds.. Grand Rapids: Kregel Academic, 2008.

Lapide, Pinchas. *The Resurrection of Jesus*. London: SPCK, 1984.

La Rondelle, Hans K. *The Israel of God in Prophecy: Principle of Prophetic Interpretation*. Berrien Springs, MI: Andrews University Press, 1983.

Larsen, David. *Jews, Gentiles and the Church: A New Perspective on History*. Grand Rapids: Discovery House, 1955.

Lutzer, Erwin W. *Hitler's Cross: The Revealing Story of How the Cross of Christ Was Used as a Symbol of the Nazi Agenda*. Chicago: Moody, 1995.

Maier, Paul L. *Josephus: The Essential Works*. Grand Rapids: Kregel, 1988, 1994.

Murphy, Catherine M. *John The Baptist: Prophet of Purity for a New Age*. Collegeville, MN: Liturgical Press, 2003.

Noah, Shmuel Ben. *Christian Replacement Theology and the Third Temple of Jerusalem*. Roma: Verlag, 2012.

Pritz, Ray, "Replacing the Jews in Early Christian Theology," *Mishkan* 21.2 (1994): 21-27.

Rausch, David A. *Fundamentalist-Evangelicals and Anti-Semitism*. Valley Forge, PA: Trinity Press International, 1993.

Rosenzweig, Franz. *The Star of Redemption*. Boston: Beacon, 1972.

Shanks, Hershel, ed. *Partings: How Judaism and Christianity Became Two.* Washington, D.C.: Biblical Archeology Society, 2013.

_____ ed. *Christianity and Rabbinic Judaism: A Parallel History of their Origins and Early Development.* 2nd ed. Washington, D.C.: Biblical Archaeology Society, 2011.

Siler, Jeffrey S. *Disinheriting the Jews: Abraham in Early Christian Controversy.* Louisville, KY: Westminster/John Knox, 1991.

Skarsaune, Oskar, and Reidar Halvik, eds. *The Early Christian Centuries: Jewish Believers in Jesus.* Peabody, MA: Hendrickson, 2007.

Stern, David. *Restoring the Jewishness of the Gospel.* Clarksville, MD: Messianic Jewish Resources International, 1988.

Vlach, Michael J. *Has the Church as a Replacement of Israel: A Theological Evaluation.* Nashville, TN: B & H, 2010.

Walker P. W. L., ed. *Jerusalem: Past and Present in the Purposes of God.* Cambridge: Tyndale House, 1992.

Watson, William C. *Dispensationalism before Darby: Seventeenth-Century and Eighteenth-Century English Apocalypticism.* Silverton, OR: Lampion Press, 2015.

Wilson, Marvin R. *Our Father Abraham: Jewish Roots of the Christian Faith.* Grand Rapids: Eerdmans, 2000.

_____. *Exploring Our Hebraic Heritage: A Christian Theology of Roots and Renewal.* Grand Rapids, MI: Eerdmans, 2014.